The
POEMS AND PLAYS
of
William Vaughn Moody

WITH AN INTRODUCTION BY

JOHN M. MANLY

VOL. II

PROSE PLAYS

BOSTON AND NEW YORK

HOUGHTON MIFFLIN COMPANY

The Riverside Press Cambridge

CONTENTS

THE GREAT DIVIDE

A Play in Three Acts

TO
HENRY MILLER
IN GRATITUDE AND FRIENDSHIP
THIS BOOK IS DEDICATED

PERSONS OF THE PLAY

PHILIP JORDAN
POLLY JORDAN, *Philip's wife*
MRS. JORDAN, *his mother*
RUTH JORDAN, *his sister*
WINTHROP NEWBURY
DR. NEWBURY, *Winthrop's father*
STEPHEN GHENT
LON ANDERSON
BURT WILLIAMS
DUTCH
A MEXICAN
A CONTRACTOR
AN ARCHITECT
A BOY

ACT I

ACT I

*Interior of Philip Jordan's cabin in southern Arizona,
on a late afternoon in spring. A large room rudely
built, adorned with blankets, pottery, weapons, and
sacred images of the local Indian tribes, and hung
with trophies of the chase, together with hunting-
knives, saddles, bridles, nose-bags for horses, lariats,
and other paraphernalia of frontier life. Through
a long low window at the back the desert is seen,
intensely colored, and covered with the uncouth shapes
of giant cacti, dotted with bunches of gorgeous bloom.
The entrance door is on the left (from the spectator's
standpoint), in a projecting elbow of the room; farther
to the left is a door leading to the sleeping-quarters.
On the right is a cook-stove, a cupboard for dishes
and household utensils, and a chimney-piece, over
which hangs a bleached cow's-skull supporting a
rifle.*

*At a rude table in the centre sits Philip Jordan, a man
of thirty-four, mending a bridle. Polly, his wife,
kneels before an open trunk, assisted in her packing by Winthrop Newbury, a recent graduate of an
Eastern medical college. Ruth Jordan, Philip's sister, a girl of nineteen, stands at the window looking
out.*

WINTHROP.

As he hands the last articles to Polly.

What on earth possessed you to bring such a load of duds to Arizona?

POLLY.

They promised me a good time, meaning one small shindig — one — in the three months I've spent in this unholy place.

Philip makes an impatient movement with the bridle; speaks gruffly.

PHILIP.

You'd better hurry. It's getting late.

RUTH.

From the window.

It's getting cooler, which is more to the point. We can make the railroad easily by sunrise, with this delicious breeze blowing.

POLLY.

Gives the finishing touches to the trunk and locks the lid.

There, at last! Heaven help the contents.

PHILIP.

Gruffly, as he rises.

Give me a lift with the trunk, Win.

They carry the trunk outside. Polly, with the aid of a cracked mirror, puts on her travelling hat and cloak.

RUTH.

My, Pollikins! You'll be the talk of all the jack-rabbits and sage hens between here and the railroad.

POLLY.

Phil is furious at me for going, and it *is* rather mean to sneak off for a visit in a grand house in San Francisco, when you poor dears have to slave on here. But really, I can't endure this life a day longer.

RUTH.

It is n't in nature that you should. Fancy *that* (*she indicates Polly with a grandiose gesture*) nourishing itself on salt-pork, chickory beans, and air-tight!

POLLY.

Do you really mean to say that apart from your pride in helping your brother, making the project go, and saving the family fortunes, you really *enjoy* yourself here?

RUTH.

Since Phil and I came out, one day has been more radiantly exciting than the other. I don't know what's the matter with me. I think I shall be punished for being so happy.

POLLY.

Punished for being happy! There's your simon-pure New-Englander.

RUTH.

True! I was discovered at the age of seven in the garret, perusing "The Twelve Pillars and Four Cornerstones of a Godly Life."

POLLY.

Pointing at Ruth's heart, speaks with mock solemnity.

If Massachusetts and Arizona ever get in a mixup in there, woe be! — Are you ever going to have that coffee done?

RUTH.

I hope soon, before you get me analyzed out of existence.

POLLY.

As Ruth busies herself at the stove.

The main point is this, my dear, and you 'd better listen to what the old lady is a-tellin' of ye. Happiness is its own justification, and it 's the sacreder the more unreasonable it is. It comes or it does n't, that 's all you can say about it. And when it comes, one has the sense to grasp it or one has n't. There you have the Law and the Prophets.

Winthrop and Philip enter from outside. Ruth, who has set out the coffee and sandwiches on the table, bows elaborately, with napkin over arm.

RUTH.

Messieurs et Mesdames!

WINTHROP.

Coffee! Well, rather, with an all-night ride in the desert ahead of us.

They drink their coffee, Philip standing sullenly apart.

Where do we get our next feed?

RUTH.

With luck, at Cottonwood Wash.

WINTHROP.

And how far may Cottonwood Wash be?

RUTH.

Thirty miles.

WINTHROP.

Sarcastically.

Local measurement?

POLLY.

Poking Philip.

Phil, for Heaven's sake say something. You diffuse the gloom of the Pit.

PHILIP.

I 've had my say out, and it makes absolutely no impression on you.

POLLY.

It 's the impression on the public I 'm anxious about.

PHILIP.

The public will have to excuse me.

POLLY.

I *am* horribly sorry for you two poor dears, left alone in this dreadful place. When Dr. Newbury goes, I don't see how you'll support life. I should like to know how long this sojourn in the wilderness is going to last, anyhow.

During the following, Ruth takes a candle from the shelf, lights it, and brings it to the table. The sunset glow has begun to fade.

RUTH.

Till Cactus Fibre makes our eternal fortune.

WINTHROP.

And how long will that be?

RUTH.

Counts on her fingers.

Two years to pay back the money we raised on mother's estate, two years of invested profits, two years of hard luck and marking time, two years of booming prosperity. Say eight years!

POLLY.

Shades of the tomb! How long do you expect to live?

RUTH.

Forever!

The sound of a galloping horse is heard, muffled by the sand.

WINTHROP.

Listen. What's that?

A boy of fifteen, panting from his rapid ride, appears at the open door.

PHILIP.

Rising and going toward the door.

What's the matter?

BOY.

I've come for the doctor.

PHILIP.

Who wants a doctor?

BOY.

Your man Sawyer, over to Lone Tree. — He's broke his leg.

RUTH.

Broken his leg! Sawyer? Our foreman?

PHILIP.

There's a nice piece of luck!—How did it happen?

BOY.

They was doin' some Navajo stunts on horse-back, pullin' chickens out of the sand at a gallop and takin' a hurdle on the upswing. Sawyer's horse renigged, and lunged off agin a 'dobe wall. Smashed his leg all to thunder.

Winthrop looks vaguely about for his kit and travelling necessaries, while Polly gives the boy food, which he accepts shyly as he goes outside with Philip. Ruth has snatched saddle and bridle from their peg.

RUTH.

I'll have Buckskin saddled for you in a jiffy. How long will it take you to set the leg?

WINTHROP.

Perhaps an hour, perhaps three.

RUTH.

It's a big détour, but you can catch us at Cottonwood Wash by sunrise, allowing three hours for Sawyer. Buckskin has done it before.

She goes out.

POLLY.

Pouting.

This will spoil all our fun! Why can't the creature wait till you get back?

WINTHROP.

Did you ever have a broken leg?

POLLY.

Well, no, not exactly a leg. But I 've had a broken
heart! In fact, I 've got one now, if you 're not
going with us.

WINTHROP.

To tell you the truth, mine is broken too.
Pause.

Did you ever dream of climbing a long hill, and
having to turn back before you saw what was
on the other side?

Polly nods enthusiastically.

I feel as if I 'd had my chance to-night to see
what was over there, and lost it.

POLLY.

You 'll excuse me if it sounds personal, Dr. Newbury, but did you expect to discern a — sort of central figure in the outrolled landscape?

WINTHROP.

Embarrassed, repenting of his sentimental outburst.

No. That is —

POLLY.

With a sweep of her arm.

O, I see. Just scenery!

She laughs and goes into the inner room, left. Ruth reënters. The sky has partly faded and a great full moon begins to rise.

RUTH.

Buckskin is ready, and so is the moon. The boy knows the trails like an Indian. He will bring you through to Cottonwood by daylight.

WINTHROP.

Taking heart.

We shall have the ride back together, at any rate.

RUTH.

Yes. — I would go with you, and try to do something to make poor Sawyer comfortable, but we have n't another horse that can do the distance.

She holds out her hand.

Good-bye.

WINTHROP.

Detaining her hand.

Won't you make it up to me?

He draws her toward him.

RUTH.

Gently but firmly.

No, Win. Please not.

WINTHROP.

Never?

RUTH.

Life is so good just as it is! Let us not change it.

He drops her hand, and goes out, without looking back. Polly reënters. The women wave Winthrop goodbye.

POLLY.

Takes Ruth by the shoulders and looks at her severely.

Conscience clear?

RUTH.

Humoring her.

Crystal!

POLLY.

Counts on her fingers.

Promising young physician, charming girl, lonely ranch, horseback excursions, spring of the year!

RUTH.

Not guilty.

POLLY.

Gracious! Then it's not play, it's earnest.

RUTH.

Neither the one nor the other. It's just your little blonde romantic noddle.

She takes Polly's head between her hands and shakes it as if to show its emptiness.

Do you think if I wanted to flirt, I would select a youth I've played hookey with, and seen his mother spank?

Suddenly sobered.

Poor dear Win! He's so good, so gentle and

chivalrous. But — (*with a movement of lifted arms, as if for air*) ah me, he's — finished! I want one that is n't finished!

POLLY.

Are you out of your head, you poor thing?

RUTH.

You know what I mean well enough. Winthrop is all rounded off, a completed product. But the man I sometimes see in my dreams is — (*pausing for a simile*) — well, like this country out here, don't you know —?

She breaks off, searching for words, and makes a vague outline in the air, to indicate bigness and incompletion.

POLLY.

Drily.

Yes, thank you. I do know! Heaven send you joy of him!

RUTH

Heaven won't, because, alas, he does n't exist! I am talking of a sublime abstraction — of the glorious unfulfilled — of the West — the Desert.

POLLY.

Lifts Ruth's chin, severely.

We have n't by chance, some spring morning, riding over to the trading-station or elsewhere — just by the merest chance *beheld* a sublime abstraction — say in blue overalls and jumper?

Ruth shakes her head.

Honest?

More emphatic head-shaking. Polly drops Ruth's chin with a shrug of the shoulders. Philip enters.

RUTH.

Putting on her riding-hat.

Is Pinto saddled?

PHILIP.

Pinto is gone.

RUTH.

Astonished.

Gone where?

PHILIP.

To that Mexican blow-out over at Lone Tree. Every man-jack on the ranch has disappeared, without leave asked or notice given, except this paper which I just found nailed to the factory door.

Ruth takes the note and reads it anxiously. Then she slowly removes her hat and lays it away.

What are you up to now? We've no time to lose!

RUTH.

With quiet determination.

I am not going.

POLLY.

As Philip turns in surprise.

Not going?

RUTH.

I must stay and look after the ranch.

PHILIP.

O, come, that's out of the question!

RUTH.

We have put all mother's money into this venture. We can't take any risks.

PHILIP.

The men will be back to-morrow. It 's not to be thought of — your staying here all alone.

POLLY.

Seats herself with decision.

One thing is certain: either Ruth goes or I stay.

PHILIP.

Takes off his hat and sets down the provision basket.

That suits me perfectly!

POLLY.

Hysterical.

But I can't stay! I won't stay! I shall go mad if I spend another night in this place.

RUTH.

No, you must n't stay. You would never get us worked up to the point of letting you go, another time.

She lifts Polly, and with arm around her waist leads her to the door.

PHILIP.

I refuse to leave you here alone, just to satisfy a whim of Polly's. That 's flat!

RUTH.

But, Phil, you forget the stores you 're to fetch
back. They will be dumped out there on the
naked sand, and by to-morrow night —

She blows across her palm, as if scattering thistledown.

PHILIP.

Well, what of it? A few hundred dollars' worth
of stuff!

RUTH.

A few hundred dollars means sink or swim with us
just now. — Besides, there 's poor Sawyer. He 'll
be brought back here to-morrow, and nobody to
nurse him. Then inflammation, fever, and good-
bye Sawyer.

*Philip, with a gesture of accepting the inevitable, picks
up the grain-sacks and basket.*

POLLY.

At the door, embracing Ruth.

Good-bye, dear. Are n't you really afraid to stay?

RUTH.

I 'm awfully sorry to miss the fun, but as for

danger, the great Arizona Desert is safer than Beacon Hill.

POLLY.

You 're sure?

RUTH.

If marauders prowl, I 'll just fire the blunderbuss out the window, and they won't stop running this side of the Great Divide.

POLLY.

Kissing her.

Good-bye, dear.

RUTH.

Good-bye.

Polly goes out.

PHILIP.

Pausing beside Ruth, at the door.

Mind you put out the light early. It can be seen from the Goodwater trail. There 's no telling what riff-raff will be straggling back that way after the dance.

RUTH.

Riff-raff! They're my sworn knights and bro-thers.

PHILIP.

In that case, what makes you uneasy about the property?

RUTH.

O, property! That's different.

PHILIP.

Well, you mind what I say and put out the light.

RUTH.

Yours for prudence!

She puts her arm around his waist and draws him to her, kissing him tenderly.

Good-bye, Phil.

He kisses her and starts to go. She still detains him. When she speaks again, her voice is softened and awed.

What a lovely night! Who would ever think to call this a desert, this moonlit ocean of flowers? What millions of cactus blooms have opened since yesterday!

PHILIP.

Looking at her dubiously.

What's the matter with you to-night?

RUTH.

Nothing. Everything. Life!— I don't know what's got into me of late. I'm just drunk with happiness the whole time.

PHILIP.

Well, you're a queer one. — Good-bye. I shall get back as soon as horseflesh will do it.

He goes out.

RUTH.

As the rumble of the wagon is heard.

Good-bye! Good-bye, Pollikins! Good-bye!

She takes the candle from the table and stands in the door for a time, then raises the light in one hand and waves her handkerchief with the other. She sets the candle again on the table, goes to the mantel-shelf, and takes down a photograph.

Dear Win! I forgot how disappointed *you* were going to be.

Pause, during which she still gazes at the picture.

Clear, kind heart!

After a moment she replaces it brusquely on the mantel-shelf, and raises her arms above her head with a deep breath. She stands thus, with arms crossed behind her head, looking at the photograph. Her gaze becomes amused and mischievous; she points her finger at the picture and whispers mockingly.

Finished! Finished!

She begins to prepare for bed, taking down her hair, and re-coiling it loosely during the following. She hums a tune vaguely and in snatches, then with a stronger rhythm; at last she sings.

> Heart, wild heart,
> Brooding apart,
> Why dost thou doubt, and why art thou sullen?
> Flower and bird
> Wait but thy word —

She breaks off, picks up a photograph from the table, and looks at it for a moment in silence.

Poor little mother! You look out at me with such patient, anxious eyes. There are better days coming for you, and it's troublesome me that's bringing them. Only you trust me!

A man's face appears at the edge of the window, gazing stealthily in. As Ruth turns, he disappears. She lays down the picture and sings again.

This is the hour,
And thine is the power.
Heart, high heart, be brave to begin it.
Dare you refuse?
Think what we lose!
Think what we gain —

The words grow indistinct as she takes up the candle
and passes into the other room, from which her voice
sounds from time to time in interrupted song. The
man again appears, shading his face with a peaked
Mexican hat so as to see into the darkened room. He
turns and waves his hand as if signalling distant
persons to approach, then enters through the open
door. He looks cautiously about the room, tiptoes to
the inner door and listens, then steals softly out, and
is seen again at the window, beckoning. Ruth reën-
ters, carrying the candle. She is shod in moccasins,
and clad in a loose, dark sleeping-dress, belted at the
waist, with wide, hanging sleeves and open throat.
As she crosses to the table she sings.

Heart which the cold
Long did enfold —
Hark, from the dark eaves the night thaw drum-
meth!
Now as a god,
Speak to the sod,
Cry to the sky that the miracle cometh!

She passes her hand over a great bunch of wild flowers on the table.

Be still, you beauties! You'll drive me to distraction with your color and your odor. I'll take a hostage for your good behavior.

She selects a red flower, puts it in the dark mass of her hair, and looks out at the open door.

What a scandal the moon is making, out there in that great crazy world! Who but me could think of sleeping on such a night?

She sits down, folds the flowers in her arms, and buries her face in them. After a moment she starts up, listens, goes hurriedly to the door, and peers out. She then shuts and bolts the door, draws the curtains before the window, comes swiftly to the table, and blows out the light. The room is left in total darkness. There are muttering voices outside, the latch is tried, then a heavy lunge breaks the bolt. A man pushes in, but is hurled back by a taller man, with a snarling oath. A third figure advances to the table, and strikes a match. As soon as the match is lighted Ruth levels the gun, which she has taken from its rack above the mantel. There is heard the click of the hammer, as the gun misses fire. It is instantly struck from her hand by the first man (Dutch), who attempts to seize her. She evades him, and tries to wrest a pistol from a holster on the wall. She is met by the second man

(Shorty), who frustrates the attempt, pocketing the weapon. While this has been going on the third man (Ghent) has been fumbling with the lamp, which he has at last succeeded in lighting. All three are dressed in rude frontier fashion; the one called Shorty is a Mexican half-breed, the others are Americans. Ghent is younger than Dutch, and taller, but less powerfully built. All are intoxicated, but not sufficiently so to incapacitate them from rapid action. The Mexican has seized Ruth and attempts to drag her toward the inner room. She breaks loose, and flies back again to the chimney-place, where she stands at bay. Ghent remains motionless and silent by the table, gazing at her.

DUTCH.

Uncorking a whiskey flask.

Plucky little catamount. I drink its health.

Drinks.

RUTH.

What do you want here?

DUTCH.

Laughs, with sinister relish.

Did you hear that, Steve?

He drinks again, and reaches out the flask to Ruth.

Take one, and pull in its purty little claws, eh? Jolly time. No more fuss and fury.

Ruth reaches for a knife, hidden behind the elbow of the chimney. Dutch wrests the knife from her and seizes her in his arms.

Peppery little devil!

With desperate strength she breaks from his clutch and reels from him in sickness of horror. Ghent remains gazing at her in a fascinated semi-stupor. Meanwhile, after closing the door, the Mexican has taken dice from his pocket, and, throwing them into a small vase on the table, shakes them and holds out the vase to Dutch. He takes it and turns to Ghent; the latter has moved a step or two toward Ruth, who in her retreat has reached the chimney-piece and stands at bay.

DUTCH.

Come, get into the game, curse you, Steve! This is going to be a free-for-all, by God!

As he rattles the dice, Ruth makes a supplicating gesture to Ghent.

RUTH.

Save me! save me!

Her gesture is frozen by his advancing towards her. She looks wildly about, shrinking from him, then with sudden desperate resolution speaks.

Save me, and I will make it up to you!

Ghent again advances; she goes on pantingly, as she stands at bay.

Don't touch me! Listen! Save me from these others, and from yourself, and I will pay you— with my life.

GHENT.

With dull wonder.

With — your life?

RUTH.

With all that I am or can be.

GHENT.

What do you mean? —
Pause.

You mean you 'll go along with me out of this? Stick to me — on the square?

RUTH.

In a tragic whisper.

Yes.

GHENT.

On the dead square?

RUTH.

Yes.

GHENT.

You won't peach, and spoil it?

RUTH.

No.

Pause, during which he looks at her fixedly.

GHENT.

Give me your hand on it!

She gives him her hand. The other men, at the table, have drawn their weapons, and hold them carelessly, but alert to the slightest suspicious movement on the part of Ghent.

DUTCH.

As Ghent turns to them.

Shorty and me 's sittin' in this game, and interested, eh, Shorty?

The Mexican nods. Ghent comes slowly to the table, eyeing the two.

Dutch holds out the vase containing the dice.

Shake for her!

GHENT.

Shake how?

DUTCH.

Any damn way! Sole and exclusive rights. License to love and cherish on the premises!

Ghent takes the vase, shakes the dice meditatively, is about to throw, then sets the vase down. He searches through his pockets and produces a few bills and a handful of silver, which he lays on the table.

GHENT.

There's all I 've got in my clothes. Take it, and give me a free field, will you?

DUTCH.

Leaning over the table to Ghent, in plaintive remonstrance.

You don't mean me, Steve!

GHENT.

To the Mexican.

Well, you, then!

The Mexican spreads the money carelessly with his left hand to ascertain its amount, then thrusts it away with a disgusted grunt of refusal.

DUTCH.

Don't blame you, Shorty! A ornery buck of a dirt-eatin' Mojave 'd pay more 'n that for his squaw.

Ruth covers her face shudderingly. Ghent stands pondering, watching the two men under his brows, and slowly gathering up the money. As if on a sudden thought, he opens his shirt, and unwinds from his neck a string of gold nuggets in the rough, strung on a leather thread.

GHENT.

Well, it ain't much, that 's sure. But there 's a string of gold nuggets I guess is worth some money.

He throws it on the table, speaking to both men.

Take that, and clear out.

DUTCH.

Draws up angrily.

I 've give you fair warning!

GHENT.

We 'll keep everything friendly between me and you. A square stand-up shoot, and the best man takes her.

DUTCH.

Mollified.

Now you 're comin' to!

GHENT.

To the Mexican.

Then it 's up to you, and you 'd better answer quick!

THE MEXICAN.

Eyeing Ghent and Ruth, points to the gun lying on the floor.

I take him, too.

GHENT.

No, you don't. You leave everything here the way you found it.

THE MEXICAN.

Alla right.

He pockets the chain and starts for the door.

GHENT.

Hold on a minute. You 've got to promise to tie the man who falls, on his horse, and take him to Mesa Grande. Bargain?

The Mexican nods.

And mouth shut, mind you, or —

He makes a sign across his throat.

THE MEXICAN.

Nods.

Alla right.

He goes out.

GHENT.

Motioning toward the door.

Outside.

DUTCH.

Surprised.

What for?

GHENT.

Sternly.

Outside!

They move toward the door. Dutch stops and waves his hand to Ruth.

DUTCH.

Don't worry, my girl. Back soon.

GHENT.

Threateningly.

Cut that out!

DUTCH.

What's eatin' you? She ain't yours yet, and I guess she won't be, not till hell freezes over.

He taps his pistol and goes out. Ghent picks up the rifle which has previously missed fire ; he unloads it, throws it on the window-seat, and follows Dutch. Ruth stands beside the table, listening. Four shots are heard. After a short time Ghent appears and watches from the door the vanishing horses. He comes to the table opposite Ruth.

RUTH.

In a low voice.

Is he dead?

GHENT.

No; but he'll stay in the coop for a while.

She sinks down in a chair. Ghent seats himself at the other side of the table, draws a whiskey flask from his pocket, and uncorks it awkwardly, using only his right hand.

RUTH.

As he is about to drink

Don't!

GHENT.

Lowers the bottle and looks at her in a dazed way.

Is this on the square?

RUTH.

I gave you my promise.

Gazing at her, he lets the bottle sink slowly by his side; the liquor runs out, while he sits as if in a stupor. Ruth glances toward the door, and half starts from her seat, sinking back as he looks up.

GHENT.

Give me a drink of water.

She brings the water from a bucket in the corner. He sets the empty bottle on the table, drinks deeply of the water, takes a handkerchief from his neck, wets it, and mops his face.

GHENT.

Where are your folks?

RUTH.

My brother has gone out to the railroad.

GHENT.

Him and you ranching it here by yourselves?

RUTH.

Yes.

GHENT.

Write him a note.

He shoves paper, pen, and ink before her.

Fix it up anyway you like.

RUTH.

Tell me first what you mean to do with me.

GHENT.

Ponders awhile in silence.

Have you got a horse to ride?

RUTH.

Yes.

GHENT.

We can reach San Jacinto before sun-up. Then we're off for the Cordilleras. I've got a claim tucked away in them hills that'll buy you the city of Frisco some day, if you have a mind to it!

She shrinks and shudders.

What you shivering at?

Ruth does not answer, but begins to write. Ghent, still using only one hand, takes a pistol from his pocket, examines it, and lays it carelessly on the table, within Ruth's reach. He rises and goes to the fireplace, takes a cigarette from his pocket and lights it, and examines the objects on the mantel-shelf. Ruth stops writing, takes up the pistol, then lays it down, as he speaks without turning round.

Read what you 've written.

Ruth, about to read, snatches up the pistol again, rises, and stands trembling and irresolute.

Why don't you shoot?

He turns round deliberately.

You promised on the square, but there 's nothing square about this deal. You ought to shoot me like a rattlesnake!

RUTH.

I know that.

GHENT.

Then why don't you?

RUTH.

Slowly.

I don't know.

GHENT.

I guess you've got nerve enough, for that or anything. — Answer me; why not?

RUTH.

I don't — know. — You laid it there for me. — And — you have no right to die.

GHENT.

How's that?

RUTH.

You must live — to pay for having spoiled your life.

GHENT.

Do you think it is spoiled?

RUTH.

Yes.

GHENT.

And how about your life?

RUTH.

I tried to do it.

GHENT.

To do what?

RUTH.

To take my life. I ought to die. I have a right to die. But I cannot, I cannot! I love my life, I must live. In torment, in darkness — it does n't matter. I want my life. I will have it!

She drops the weapon on the table, pushes it toward him, and covers her eyes.

Take it away! Don't let me see it. If you want me on these terms, take me, and may God forgive you for it; but if there is a soul in you to be judged, don't let me do myself violence.

She sinks down by the table, hiding her face in her hands.

O, God have pity on me!

Ghent puts the pistol back into his belt, goes slowly to the outer door, opens it, and stands for some moments gazing out. He then closes the door, and takes a step or two toward the table. As he speaks, Ruth's sobs cease, she raises her head and looks strangely at him.

GHENT.

I've lived hard and careless, and lately I've been going down hill pretty fast. But I have n't got so low yet but what I can tell one woman from another. If that was all of it, I'd be miles away from here by now, riding like hell for liquor to wash the taste of shame out of my mouth. But that ain't all. I've seen what I've been looking the world over for, and never knew it. — Say your promise holds, and I 'll go away now.

RUTH.

O, yes, go, go! You will be merciful. You will not hold me to my cruel oath.

GHENT.

And when I come back?
Ruth does not answer. He takes a step nearer.
And when I come back?

RUTH.

You never — could — come back.

GHENT.

No, I guess I never could.

RUTH.
Eager, pleading.
You *will* go?

GHENT.

For good?

RUTH.

Yes.

GHENT.

Do you mean that?

RUTH.

Wildly.

Yes, yes, ten thousand times!

GHENT.

Is that your last word?

RUTH.

Yes.

Pause. She watches him with strained anxiety.

O, why did you come here to-night?

GHENT.

I come because I was blind-drunk and sun-crazy, and looking for damnation the nearest way. That's why I come. But that's not why I'm staying. I'm talking to you in my right mind now. I want you to try and see this thing the way it is.

RUTH.

O, that is what I want you to do! You did yourself and me a hideous wrong by coming here. Don't do us both a more hideous wrong still! I was in panic fear. I snatched at the first thing I could. Think what our life would be, beginning as we have begun! O, for God's pity go away now, and never come back! Don't you see there can never be anything between us but hatred, and misery, and horror?

GHENT.

Hardening.

We'll see about that! — Are you ready to start?

Ruth, conscious for the first time of her undress condition, shrinks, and folds her gown closer about her neck.

Go, and be quick about it.

She starts toward her room; he detains her.

Where's your saddle?

She points at it and goes out. Ghent picks up the note she has written, reads it, and stands for a moment in reflection before laying it down. He gets more water from the bucket, drinks deeply, mops his face, and rolls up the sleeve of his left arm, which is soaked with blood. He tries awkwardly to stanch a wound in his forearm, gives it up in disgust, and rolls down his sleeve again. He reads the note once more, then takes Ruth's saddle and bridle from the wall and goes out. Ruth comes in; her face is white and haggard, but her manner determined and collected. She comes to the table, and sees the bloody handkerchief and basin of water. As Ghent enters, she turns to him anxiously.

RUTH.

You are hurt.

GHENT.

It 's no matter.

RUTH.

Where?

He indicates his left arm. She throws off her hooded riding-cloak, and impulsively gathers together water, towels, liniment, and bandages; she approaches him, quite lost in her task, flushed and eager.

Sit down. — Roll up your sleeve.

He obeys mechanically. She rapidly and deftly washes and binds the wound, speaking half to herself, between long pauses.

Can you lift your arm? — The bone is not

touched. — It will be all right in a few days. —
This balsam is a wonderful thing to heal.

GHENT.

Watching her dreamily, as she works.

What's your name?

RUTH.

Ruth — Ruth — Jordan.

Long pause.

There, gently. — It must be very painful.

He shakes his head slowly, with half-humorous protest.

GHENT.

It's not fair!

RUTH.

What is n't fair?

GHENT.

To treat me like this. It's not in the rules of the
game.

RUTH.

As the sense of the situation again sweeps over her.

Binding your wound? I would do the same service for a dog.

GHENT.

Yes, I dare say. But the point is, I ain't a dog; I'm a human — the worst way!

She rises and puts away the liniment and bandages. He starts up, with an impulsive gesture.

Make this bad business over into something good for both of us! You'll never regret it! I'm a strong man!

He holds out his right arm, rigid.

I used to feel sometimes, before I went to the bad, that I could take the world like that and tilt her over. And I can do it, too, if you say the word! I'll put you where you can look down on the proudest. I'll give you the kingdoms of the world and all the glory of 'em.

She covers her face with her hands. He comes nearer.

Give me a chance, and I'll make good. By God, girl, I'll make good! — I'll make a queen of you. I'll put the world under your feet!

Ruth makes a passionate gesture, as if to stop her ears.

What makes you put your hands over your ears like that? Don't you like what I'm saying to you?

RUTH.

Taking the words with difficulty.

Do you remember what that man said just now?

GHENT.

What about?

RUTH.

About the Indian — and — his squaw.

GHENT.

Yes. There was something in it, too. I was a fool to offer him that mean little wad.

RUTH.

For — me!

GHENT.

Well, yes, for you, if you want to put it that way.

RUTH.

But — a chain of nuggets — that comes nearer being a fair price?

GHENT.

O, to buy off a greaser!

RUTH.

But to buy the soul of a woman — one must go higher. A mining-claim! The kingdoms of the world and all the glory of them!

Breaking down in sudden sobs.

O, be careful how you treat me! Be careful! I say it as much for your sake as mine. Be careful!

GHENT.

Turns from her, his bewilderment and discomfiture translating itself into gruffness.

Well, I guess we 'll blunder through. — Come along! We 've no time to lose. — Where are your things?

At her gesture, he picks up the saddle-pack which she has brought out of the bedroom with her, and starts toward the door.

RUTH.

Taking a hammer from the window-ledge and handing it to Ghent.

Fix the bolt. My brother must not know.

He drives in the staple of the bolt, while she throws the blood-stained water and handkerchief into the fire. He aids her in replacing the weapons on the walls, then takes the saddle-pack and stands at the door, waiting. She picks up her mother's picture, and thrusts it in her bosom. After standing a moment in hesitation, she takes the picture out, kisses it, lays it on the mantel, face down. She extinguishes the lamp, and goes out hastily. He follows, closing the door.

THE CURTAIN FALLS IN DARKNESS

ACT II

ACT II

*Stephen Ghent's home, in the Cordilleras. At the right,
crowning a rude terrace, is an adobe cabin, stained
a pale buff, mellowed to ivory by sun and dust.
Over it clamber vines loaded with purple bloom. The
front of the cabin is turned at an angle toward
the spectator, the farther side running parallel with
the brink of a cañon, of which the distant wall and
upper reaches are crimsoned by the afternoon light.
In the level space before the rocky terrace is a stone
table and seats, made of natural rocks roughly worked
with the chisel. The rude materials have manifestly
been touched by a refined and artistic hand, bent on
making the most of the glorious natural background.
Against the rocks on the left stands a large hand-loom
of the Navajo type, with weaving-stool, and a blanket
half woven. On the table lies a half-finished Indian
basket, and strips of colored weaving-materials lie in
a heap on the ground. Cactus plants in blossom fill
the niches of the rocks and lift their fantastic forms
above the stones which wall the cañon brink. At one
point this wall is broken, where a path descends into
the cañon.*

*Lon Anderson, a venerable-looking miner, with gray
hair and beard, sits smoking before the cabin. Burt
Williams, a younger man, peeps up over the edge of
the cañon, from the path.*

BURT.

Hello, Lon. Is the Missus inside?

Lon smokes on, without looking at the questioner.

Look here, I put a nickel in you, you blame rusty old slot-machine. Push out something!

LON.

Removes his pipe deliberately.

What you wantin' off 'n her now? A music lesson or a headache powder?

BURT.

Boss 's waitin' down at the mine, with a couple o' human wonders he 's brought back with him from wherever he 's been this time. Something doin' on the quiet.

LON.

You can tell him his wife ain't nowheres about.

Burt produces an enormous bandana from his pocket, mounts the wall, and waves it. He sits on the wall and smokes for a moment in silence, looking down into the cañon, as if watching the approaching party. He points with his pipe at the cabin.

BURT.

Funny hitch-up — this here one — I think.

LON.

After a pause.

How much you gittin' a day now?

BURT.

Same little smilin' helpless three and six-bits.

LON.

Anything extry for thinkin'?

BURT.

Nope! Throwed in.

*They smoke again. Burt glances down to reassure him-
self, then points at the loom and basket.*

Queer business — this rug-weavin' and basket-
makin', ain't it? — What d' ye s'pose she wants
to sit, day in and day out, like a half-starved
Navajo, slavin' over them fool things fur? —
Boss ain't near, is he? Don't keep her short of
ice-cream sodas and trolley-rides, does 'e?

Lon rises and approaches Burt, regarding him grimly.

Saw 'er totin' a lot o' that stuff burro-back over to the hotel week 'fore last. — An' Dod Ranger — you know what a disgustin' liar Dod is — he tells how he was makin' tests over in the cross-cañon, an' all of a sudden plump he çomes on her talkin' to a sawed-off Mexican hobo, and when she sees Dod, she turns white 's a sheet.

LON.

With suppressed ferocity.

You tell Dod Ranger to keep his mouth shet, and you keep yourn shet too — or by Jee— hosophat, I'll make the two of ye eat yer Adam's-apples and swaller the core!

BURT.

O, git down off 'n yer hind legs, Lon! Nobody 's intendin' any disrespect.

LON.

You boys keep yer blatherin' tongues off 'n her! Or you 'll get mixed up with Alonzo P. Anderson — (*he taps his breast*) — so 's it 'll take a coroner to untangle ye!

BURT.

Deprecatingly.

I guess I 'd stick up fur 'er 's quick as you would, come to that.

LON.

Well, we don't need no stickin' up fur 'er. What we need is less tongue.

He leans down and speaks lower.

Especially when the boss is round. You tell the boys so.

Burt looks at him in surprise and is about to speak; Lon makes a warning signal, indicating the approach of the party below. Burt descends, saluting Ghent respectfully.

GHENT.

Peeping up over the edge of the cañon.

Coast clear, eh, Lon?

LON.

Yes, sir.

GHENT.

Where is she?

Lon.

Points along the brink of the cañon.

Kind o' think she went out to Look-off Ledge. — Guess she did n't expect you back to-day.

Ghent.

Speaking below.

Come up, gentlemen.

Ghent emerges from the cañon, followed by an architect, a dapper young Easterner, and a contractor, a bluff Western type. Ghent is neatly dressed in khaki, with riding-boots and broad felt hat. He has a prosperous and busy air, and is manifestly absorbed in the national game of making money.

Take a seat.

Contractor.

Seats himself by the table.

Don't care if I do. That new stage of yours just jumped stiff-legged from the go-off. And the trail up here from the mine is a good deal of a proposition for the see-dentary.

Architect.

As he takes in the stupendous view.

What a wonderful place! Even better than you described it.

GHENT.

Yes. My wife picked it out. — Let's see your plans.

He removes basket from the table, where the architect unrolls several sheets of blue paper.

ARCHITECT.

I have followed your instructions to the letter. I understand that nothing is to be touched except the house.

GHENT.

Not a stone, sir; not a head of cactus. Even the vines you 've got to keep, exactly as they are.

ARCHITECT.

Smiling.

That will be a little difficult.

GHENT.

You can put 'em on a temporary trellis. — A little pains will do it.

CONTRACTOR.

Maybe, with a man to shoo the masons off with a shot-gun.

GHENT.

Over the plans.

Provide a dozen men, if necessary, with machine guns.

CONTRACTOR.

As you please, Mr. Ghent. The owner of the Verde mine has a right to his whims, I reckon.

ARCHITECT.

I have designed the whole house in the Spanish style, very broad and simple. This open space where we stand — (*points to the plans*) — I have treated as a semi-enclosed *patio*, with arcaded porches.

GHENT.

Dubiously.

Good.

ARCHITECT.

This large room fronting the main arcade is the living-room.

GHENT.

I guess we'll have 'em all living-rooms. This place is to be lived in, from the word go.

ARCHITECT.

Humoring him.

To be sure, everything cheerful and open. — Here on the left of the inner court is the library and music-room.

GHENT.

I'm afraid we won't have much use for that. My wife don't go in much for frills. I used to play the concertina once, but it was a long while ago.

ARCHITECT.

It can be used for other purposes. For instance, as a nursery, though I had put that on the other side.

GHENT.

Embarrassed and delighted.

Um, yes, nursery. — Stamping-ground for the —?

The architect nods; the contractor follows suit, with emphasis. Lon nods solemnly over his pipe.

Good.

The architect bends over to make a note with his pencil. Ghent restrains him and says somewhat sheepishly in his ear.

You can leave it music-room on the map.

ARCHITECT.

Continuing his explanation.

This wing —

Ghent, interrupting him, holds the plan at arm's length, with head on one side and eyes squinted, as he looks from the drawings to the cabin and surroundings.

GHENT.

Looks a little — *sprawly* on paper. I had sort of imagined something more — more up in the air, like them swell tepees on the Hill in Frisco.

He makes a grandiose outline of high roofs and turrets in the air.

ARCHITECT.

I think this is more harmonious with the surroundings.

CONTRACTOR.

In answer to Ghent's inquiring look.

Won't look so showy from the new hotel across yonder.

He points to the left, down the curve of the cañon wall.

GHENT.

What's your estimate on this plan, now you've seen the location?

CONTRACTOR.

It's a long way to haul the stuff. — Say some-
wheres between twenty and twenty-five thousand. Twenty-five will be safe.

GHENT.

Slightly staggered.

That's a big lot of money, my friend!

CONTRACTOR.

With cold scorn.

I thought we was talkin' about a *house!* I can
build you a good sheep-corral for a right smart
less.

GHENT.

Well, I guess we don't want any sheep-corrals.

CONTRACTOR.

I should think not, with the Verde pumping
money at you the way they tell she does.

GHENT.

*Holds up the plans again and looks at them in per-
plexed silence.*

I'll tell you, gentlemen, I'll have to consult my

wife about this before I decide. The fact is, I 've been working the thing out on the sly, up to now.

CONTRACTOR.

Expect to build it of an afternoon, while the lady was takin' her see-ester?

GHENT.

I thought I 'd smuggle her off somewhere for a while.

He is silent a moment, pondering.

No! It 's her house, and she must O. K. the plans before ground is broke.

He looks along the cañon rim.

Would you mind waiting a few minutes till I see if I can find her?

He starts irresolutely, then turns back.

Or better still, leave the plans, and I 'll see you at the hotel to-morrow morning. I have n't been over there since it was opened. I'd like to know what they 're making of it.

CONTRACTOR.

Astonished.

Hain't been over to the Buny Visty yet ?

GHENT.

Too busy.

CONTRACTOR.

Well, you 'll find it an up-to-date joint, and chock full of tourist swells and lungers.

GHENT.

Good-afternoon, gentlemen. You 'll excuse me. You can find your way back all right? Take the left-hand path. It 's better going.

The architect bows ceremoniously, the contractor nods. Ghent disappears along the cañon brink behind the cabin.

ARCHITECT.

Has been examining the work on the loom, and has then picked up the unfinished basket, admiringly.

What a beautiful pattern! I say, this is like those we saw at the hotel. (*To Lon.*) May I ask who is making this?

Lon smokes in silence; the architect raises his voice, slightly sharp.

May I ask who is making this?

LON.

Benignly.

You kin, my friend, you kin!

ARCHITECT.

Well, then, the question is put.

LON.

And very clear-put, too. You'd ought to be in the law business, young man.

He gets up deliberately.

Or some other business that'd take up all yer time.

ARCHITECT.

Between wrath and amusement.

Well, I'll be hanged!

He follows his companion down the cañon path, stopping a moment at the brink to look round with a professional air at the house and surroundings, then at Lon.

Tart old party!

He descends. Lon crosses to the table, looks over the plans, makes outlines in the air in imitation of Ghent, then shakes his head dubiously, as he rolls up the plans.

Ruth appears, emerging from the cañon path. She wears the same dress as at the close of Act I, with a dark scarf-like handkerchief thrown over her head.

She is pale and exhausted. She sinks on the rocks at the edge of the cañon.

LON.

Approaching her, anxiously.

It's too much fer you, ma'am. You'd oughter let me go.

He brings her a glass of water from an Indian water-jar before the cabin.

RUTH.

Tasting the water.

O, I thought I should never get back!

She leans against a rock, with closed eyes, then rouses herself again.

Lon, take the glass, and see if you can make out any one down yonder, on the nearer trail. I — I thought some one was following me.

LON.

Speaks low.

Excuse me askin', Mis' Ghent, but is that dod-blamed Mexican a-botherin' you again?

RUTH.

No. He has gone away, for good. It's some one I

saw at the hotel — some one I used to know. —
Look if you can make out a man's figure, coming
up.

LON.

*Takes the glass from the niche in the rocks, and scans
the cañon path.*

Can't see nothin' but a stray burro, an' he ain't
got no figger to speak of. — Might be t'other
side o' Table Rock, down in the pinyon scrub.

*Ruth gets up with an effort, takes the glass and looks
through it, then lays it on the ledge.*

Excuse me, ma'am, but — Mister Ghent come
home this afternoon.

RUTH.

Startled.

Where is he?

LON.

Huntin' for you down Look-off Ledge way. I
'lowed you was there, not knowin' what else to
say.

RUTH.

Thank you, Lon. — You can go now.

*He goes down the cañon path. Ruth looks once more
through the glass, then crosses to the table, where she*

sits down and begins to finger the roll of plans.
Ghent reënters. He approaches with soft tread and
bends over Ruth. She starts up with a little cry,
avoiding his embrace.

You frightened me. — When did you come back?

GHENT.

An hour ago.

RUTH.

Was your journey successful?

GHENT.

Yes. But my home-coming — that looks rather
like a failure.

Pause.

I expected to find you out on the bluff.

RUTH.

Lon was mistaken. I had gone the other way.

As she stands at the table, she begins to unroll the plans.

What are these papers?

GHENT.

Have n't you one word of welcome for me, after
five days?

Ruth remains silent, with averted head, absently un-
rolling the packet.

Not a look even?

He waits a moment, then sighs and seats himself moodily by the table.

I never can remember! After I 've been away from you for twelve hours, I forget completely.

RUTH.

Forget what?

GHENT.

How it stands between us. It 's childish, but for the life of me I can't help it. — After I 've been away a few hours, this place gets all lit up with bright colors in my mind, like — (*searching for a simile*) — well, like a Christmas tree! I dare say a Christmas tree don't amount to much in real life, but I saw one once, in a play, — I was a little mining-camp roust-about, so high, — and ever since it has sort of stood to me for the gates o' glory.

RUTH.

With a hysterical laugh.

A Christmas tree!

She bows her head in her hands, and repeats the words, as if to herself, in a tone in which bitterness has given place to tragic melancholy.

A Christmas tree!

Ghent, watching her moodily, crumples up the plans and throws them upon the ground. He goes toward the cabin, hesitates, turns, and comes back to the table, where Ruth still sits with buried head. He draws from his pocket a jewel-case, which he opens and lays before her.

GHENT.

There is a little present I brought home for you. And here are some more trinkets.

He takes out several pieces of jewelry and tumbles them together on the table.

I know you don't care much for these things, but I had to buy something, the way I was feeling. And these papers — (*picks them up and spreads them out on the table*) —these mean that you're not to live much longer in a mud shanty, with pine boxes for furniture. These are the drawings for a new house that I want to talk over with you.

He points at the map and speaks glibly, trying to master his discomfiture at her lack of interest.

Spanish style, everything broad and simple! Large living-room opening on inner court. Library and music-room, bless your heart. Bedrooms; kitchen and thereunto pertaining. Wing where the proprietor retires to express his inmost feelings. General effect sprawly, but harmonious with the surroundings. Twenty thousand estimated, twenty-five limit. Is she ours?

RUTH.

In a dead, flat tone.

How much did you say the house is to cost?

GHENT.

Twenty-five thousand dollars at the outside.

RUTH.

And these — trinkets?

GHENT.

O, I don't know. — A few hundred.

RUTH.

Draws the plans toward her and pours the jewels in a heap upon them from her lifted hands.

Twenty-five thousand dollars and the odd hundreds!

She laughs suddenly and jarringly.

My price has risen! My price has risen!

She laughs again, as she rises from the table and looks down the cañon path.

Keep those displayed to show to our visitors! My honor is at stake.

She points down the path.

There is one coming now!

GHENT.

Visitors? What visitors?

RUTH.

Only an old school-friend of mine; a Mr. Winthrop Newbury.

GHENT.

What are you talking about? Are you crazy?

He joins her, where she stands looking down into the cañon.

This fellow, is he really what you say?

Ruth nods, with unnaturally bright eyes and mocking smile.

What does this mean?

RUTH.

It means that he caught sight of me, an hour ago, in the hotel.

GHENT.

In the hotel? What were you doing there?

RUTH.

With biting calm.

Nothing wicked — as yet. They don't pay twenty-five thousand dollars over there — at least not yet!

Ghent turns sharply, as if stung by a physical blow. She raises her hands to him, in a swift revulsion of feeling.

O, don't judge me! Don't listen to me! I am not in my right mind.

GHENT.

Sweeps the jewels together, and throws them over the cliff.

Do you want me to be here, while you see him?

She does not answer.

Won't you answer me?

RUTH.

Again cold.

Act as you think best.

GHENT.

It's a question of what will be easiest for you.

RUTH.

O, it's all easy for me!

*Ghent stands irresolute, then raises his hand in a ges-
ture of perplexity and despair, and goes into the
house, closing the door. Winthrop Newbury appears
at the top of the cañon path, looks curiously about,
catches sight of Ruth's averted figure, and rushes
toward her.*

WINTHROP.

Ruth! Is it really you?

*Ruth starts involuntarily toward him, stretching out
her arms. As he advances, she masters herself, and
speaks in a natural voice, with an attempt at gayety,
as she takes his hand.*

RUTH.

Well, of all things! Winthrop Newbury! How
did you find your way to this eagle's nest?

WINTHROP.

I — we saw you — we caught a glimpse of you at the hotel, but we were n't sure. We followed you, but lost you in the cañon.

RUTH.

We? Who is we?

WINTHROP.

Your brother and his wife.

RUTH.

Turning the shock, which she has been unable to conceal, into conventional surprise.

Philip and Polly here!

WINTHROP.

They took the other turn, down there where the path forks. We did n't know which way you had gone.

RUTH.

Yes, but why on earth are they here at all?

WINTHROP.

They are on their way East. They stopped over to see me.

RUTH.

To see you? Are you — living here?

WINTHROP.

I have been here only a week.

He starts impulsively, trying to break through the con-
ventional wall which she has raised between them.

Ruth — for God's sake —!

RUTH.

Interrupting him, with exaggerated animation.

But tell me! I am all curiosity. How do you
happen to be here — of all places?

WINTHROP.

What does it matter? I am here. We have found
you, after all these miserable months of anxiety
and searching. O Ruth — why —

RUTH.

I have acted badly, I know. But I wish not to
talk of that. Not now. I will explain everything
later. Tell me about yourself — about Philip and
Polly — and mother. I am thirsty for news.
What have you been doing all these months, since
— our queer parting?

WINTHROP.

Solemnly.

Looking for you.

Pause.

O Ruth — how could you do it? How could you do it?

RUTH.

Touches him on the arm and looks at him with dumb entreaty, speaking low.

Winthrop!

WINTHROP.

In answer to her unspoken words.

As you will.

RUTH.

Resumes her hard, bright tone.

You have n't told me about mother. How is she?

WINTHROP.

Well. Or she will be, now. Ruth, you ought at least to have written to her. She has suffered cruelly.

RUTH.

Quickly, with a nervous uplift of her arms.

Yes, yes, I know that! — And you are — settled here? You mean to remain?

WINTHROP.

I am physician at the End-of-the-Rainbow mines, three miles below. At least I — I am making a trial of it.

Pause.

How pale and worn you are. — Don't turn away. Look at me.

She flinches, then summons her courage and looks him steadily in the face.

You are — you are ill — I fear you are desperately ill!

RUTH.

Moving away nervously.

Nonsense. I was never better in my life.

She goes toward the cañon brink.

You have n't praised our view. We are very proud of it.

WINTHROP.

Following her.

Yes, very fine. Magnificent.

RUTH.

But you 're not looking at it at all! Do you see that bit of smoke far down yonder? That is the stamp mill of the Rio Verde mine.

WINTHROP.

Compelling himself to follow her lead.

Yes — the Rio Verde. One of the big strikes of the region. Dispute about the ownership, I believe.

RUTH.

None that I ever heard of, and I ought to know. For — (*she makes a sweeping bow*) — we are the Rio Verde, at your service.

WINTHROP.

You — your — husband is the owner of the Verde mine?

RUTH.

No less!

WINTHROP.

Embarrassed.

We found the record of your marriage at San Jacinto. The name was Ghent — Stephen Ghent.

RUTH.

Yes. He will be so glad to see some of my people.

Winthrop's eyes have fallen on the basket at the foot of the table. He picks it up, examines it curiously, and looks meaningly at Ruth, who snatches it from his hand and throws it over the cliff.

A toy I play with! You know I always have to keep my hands busy pottering at some rubbishy craft or other.

WINTHROP.

Is about to speak, but checks himself. He points at the loom.

And the blanket, too?

RUTH.

Yes, another fad of mine. It is really fascinating work. The Indian women who taught me think I am a wonder of cleverness.

WINTHROP.

So do — the women — over there.

He points across the cañon.

RUTH.

Flushing.

Ah, yes, you saw some of my stuff at the hotel.
You know how vain I am. I had to show it.

WINTHROP.

Perhaps. But why should the wife of the man
who owns the Verde mine *sell* her handiwork, and
under such — such vulgar conditions?

RUTH.

Brilliantly explanatory.

To see if it *will* sell, of course! That is the test of
its merit.

*He looks at her in mute protest, then with a shake of
the head, rises and puts on his hat.*

WINTHROP.

Do you want to see the others?

RUTH.

Why, yes, to be sure I do. How should I not?

WINTHROP.

You have n't seemed very anxious — these last eight months.

RUTH.

True. I have been at fault. I so dread explanations. And Phil's tempests of rage! Poor boy, he must feel sadly ill-used.

WINTHROP.

He does.

Hesitates.

If there is any reason why you would rather he did n't see you, just now, —

RUTH.

There is no reason. At least, none valid.

WINTHROP.

Then I will bring them up.

RUTH.

By all means.

She holds out her hand, smiling.

Auf wiedersehen!

Winthrop releases her hand and goes toward the cañon path. He waves, and turns to Ruth.

WINTHROP.

They are just below.

As Ruth advances he takes her hand and looks searchingly into her eyes.

For old friendship's sake, won't you give me one human word before they come? At least answer me honestly one human question?

RUTH.

Keeping up her hard, bright gayety.

In the great lottery of a woman's answers there is always one such prize!

WINTHROP.

Dejectedly, as he drops her hand.

It's no use, if that is your mood.

RUTH.

My mood! Your old bugbear! I am as sober-serious as my stars ever let me be.

WINTHROP.

Did you, that night you bade me good-bye, know that — this was going to happen?

RUTH.

Cordially explanatory.

No. It was half accident, half wild impulse. Phil left me at the ranch alone. My lover came, impatient, importunate, and I — went with him.

WINTHROP.

And your — this man — to whom you are married — pardon me, you don't need to answer unless you wish — for how long had you known him?

RUTH.

Solemnly, as she looks him straight in the eyes.

All my life! And for æons before.

He looks at her for a moment, then goes toward the cañon path. Polly's voice is heard calling.

POLLY.

Not yet visible.

Win! Win!

WINTHROP.

Calls down the cañon.

Come up! Come up!

Ruth goes past him down the cañon path. In a moment she reappears, with Polly. They are laughing and talking as they come.

POLLY.

Ruth!

RUTH.

Dear old Polly!

POLLY.

You *naughty* girl!

RUTH.

If our sins must find us out, you are the kind of Nemesis I choose.

POLLY.

My! But you 're a shady character. And sly!

Philip appears. Ruth hurries to embrace him, while Polly, fanning herself with her handkerchief, examines the house and surroundings with curiosity.

RUTH.

O Phil! — Dear old man!

She covers his face lightly with her hands.

No scolding, no frowns. This is the finding of the prodigal, and she expects a robe and a ring.

POLLY.

Seating herself on a rock.

Heavens, what a climb! — I 'm a rag.

RUTH.

Motions to the men to be seated.

The cabin would n't hold us all, but there 's one good thing about this place; there 's plenty of outdoors.

WINTHROP.

Looking about.

I should say there was!

POLLY.

To think of our practical Ruth doing the one really theatrical thing known in the annals of Milford Corners, Mass.! — And what a setting! My dear, your stage arrangements are perfect.

RUTH.

In this case Providence deserves the credit. We may have come here to have our pictures taken, but we stayed to make a living.

Philip has drawn apart, gloomy and threatening. Polly keeps up her heroic efforts to give the situation a casual and humorous air.

POLLY.

With jaunty challenge.

Well, where is he?

RUTH.

Who?

POLLY.

He!

Ruth points at the cabin, smiling.

Well, produce him!

RUTH.

Following, with gratitude in her eyes, the key of lightness and raillery which Polly has struck.

You insist?

POLLY.

Absolutely.

RUTH.

O, very well!

She goes up the rocky incline, and enters the cabin, calling: "Steve! Steve!" Polly goes to Philip, and shakes him.

POLLY.

Now you behave!

Indicates Winthrop.

He's behaving.

Ruth reappears in the doorway, followed by Ghent.

RUTH.

With elaborate gayety, as they descend the rocks.

Well, Stephen, since they've run us to earth, I suppose we must put a good face on it, and acknowledge them. — This is Polly, of whom I've talked so much. Polly the irresistible. Beware of her!

Polly shakes his hand cordially.

And this is — my brother Philip.

Ghent extends his hand, which Philip pointedly ignores. Ruth goes on hastily, to cover the insult.

And this is my old school-friend, Winthrop Newbury.

They shake hands.

WINTHROP.

To Philip, formally explanatory.

Mr. Ghent is the owner of the famous Verde mine.

GHENT.

Part owner, sir. I had n't the capital to develop with, so I had to dispose of a half-interest.

WINTHROP.

Is n't there some litigation under way?

RUTH.

Looking at Ghent, surprised.

Litigation?

GHENT.

Yes — a whole rigmarole.

POLLY.

Catching at a straw to make talk.

Heaven help you if you have got entangled in the law! I can conceive of nothing more horrible or ghostly than a court of law; unless (*she glances at Philip*) it is that other court of high justice,

which people hold in private to judge their fellows, from hearsay and half-knowledge!

RUTH.

*Keeping up the play desperately, as she blesses Polly
with a look.*

But there must be law, just the same, and pen-
alties and rewards and all that. Else what's the
use of being good?

POLLY.

Like you — for instance!

RUTH.

Well, yes, like me!

POLLY.

You are not good, you are merely magnificent. I
want to be magnificent! I want to live on the
roof of the world and own a gold mine!

To Ghent.

Show me where the sweet thing is.

GHENT.

We can get a better view of the plant from the
ledge below. Will you go down?

*Ghent, Polly, and Winthrop go down the cañon path.
Ruth takes Philip by the arm, to lead him after.*

PHILIP.

No. We must have a word together, before the gabble begins again. Winthrop has given me your explanation, which explains nothing.

RUTH.

Trying to keep up the light tone.

Has n't that usually been the verdict on explanations of my conduct?

PHILIP.

Don't try to put me off! Tell me in two words how you came to run away with this fellow.

RUTH.

Hardening.

Remember to whom you are speaking, and about whom.

PHILIP.

I got your note, with its curt announcement of your resolve. Later, by mere accident, we found the record of your marriage at San Jacinto — if you call it a marriage, made hugger-mugger at midnight by a tipsy justice of the peace. I don't want to question its validity. I only pray that no one will. But I want to know how it came to be made, in such hurry and secrecy — how it came to be made at all, for that matter. How did you ever come to disgrace yourself and your family by clandestine meetings and a hedge-row marriage with a person of this class? And why, after the crazy leap was taken, did you see fit to hide yourself away without a word to me or your distracted mother? Though that perhaps is easier to understand!

RUTH.

The manner of your questions absolves me from the obligation to answer them.

PHILIP.

I refuse to be put off with any such patent sub-terfuge.

RUTH.

Subterfuge or not, it will have to suffice, until you remember that my right to choose my course in life is unimpeachable, and that the man whose destiny I elect to share cannot be insulted in my presence.

PHILIP.

Very well, I can wait. The truth will come out some day. Meanwhile, you can take comfort from the fact that your desertion at the critical moment of our enterprise has spelled ruin for me.

RUTH.

Overwhelmed.

Philip, you don't mean —!

PHILIP.

Absolute and irretrievable ruin.

RUTH.

Then you are going back East — for good?

PHILIP.

Yes.

RUTH.

But — mother's money! What will she do?

Philip shrugs his shoulders.

Is everything gone — everything?

PHILIP.

I shall get something from the sale. Perhaps

enough to make a fresh start, somewhere, in some small way.

RUTH.

Comes to him, and lays her arms on his shoulders.

Phil, I am sorry, sorry!

He caresses her; she bursts into suppressed convulsive weeping and clings to him, hiding her face in his breast.

PHILIP.

Ruth, you are not happy! You have made a hideous mistake. Come home with me.

Ruth shakes her head.

At least for a time. You are not well. You look really ill. Come home with us, if only for a month.

RUTH.

No, no, dear Phil, dear brother!

She draws down his face and kisses him; then lifts her head, with an attempt at lightness.

There! I have had my cry, and feel better. The excitement of seeing you all again is a little too much for me.

PHILIP.

If there is anything that you want to tell me about all this, tell me now.

RUTH.

O, there will be plenty of time for explanations and all that! Let us just be happy now in our re-union.

PHILIP.

There will not be plenty of time. We leave to-morrow morning.

RUTH.

Then you will take me on trust — like a dear good brother. Perhaps I shall never explain! I like my air of mystery.

PHILIP.

Remember that if you ever have anything to complain of — in your life — it is my right to know it. The offender shall answer to me, and dearly, too.

RUTH.

Takes his head between her hands, and shakes it, as with recovered gayety.

Of course they will, you old fire-eater!

PHILIP.

Pointing to the blanket on the loom.

Ruth, at least tell me why —.

Ruth does not see his gesture, as she is looking at the others, who come up from below. The men linger in the background, Ghent pointing out objects in the landscape.

RUTH.

To Polly, who advances.

Well, what do you think of us, in a bird's-eye view?

POLLY.

In a bird's-eye view you are superb!

She draws Ruth to her, and speaks in a lower tone.

And looked at near, you are an enthralling puzzle.

RUTH.

Half to herself.

If you only knew how much!

POLLY.

Taking Ruth by the chin as in Act I.

So you *had* — just by chance — riding over to

the trading-station or so — met the glorious
unfulfilled — in blue overalls and a jumper! I
thought so!

*Ruth bows her head in a spasm of pain. Polly, who
does not see her face, goes on teasingly.*

I see now what you meant about wanting one
that was n't finished. This one certainly is n't
finished. But when he is, he 'll be grand!

*Ruth moves away with averted head. Polly follows
her, peeping round to view her face.*

Don't sulk! I meant nothing disrespectful. On
the contrary, I 'm crazy about him.

In a louder tone.

And now that I 've seen the outside of you, I *must*
peep into that fascinating little house!

RUTH.

To Ghent, who has drawn nearer.

Polly wants to go inside the cabin. I can't let
her until we have shown her what it 's going to
be.

*With Ghent's aid she spreads out the plans, which Polly
examines with curiosity.*

These are the plans for our new house. You call

us magnificent. We will show you that we are
not. We are overwhelming!

WINTHROP.

Looking at his watch.

I am afraid we must be getting back. It grows
dark very suddenly in the cañon.

RUTH.

To Polly.

Well, then you may come in, if you will promise
to view the simple present in the light of the
ornate future.

*Polly goes in. Ruth, lingering at the door for an in-
stant, looks back anxiously at the men.*

PHILIP.

Curtly, to Ghent.

If you will permit me, I should like a word with
you.

GHENT.

Certainly.

*Winthrop effaces himself, making and lighting a cigar-
ette, as he looks out over the cañon.*

PHILIP.

In deference to my sister's wishes, I refrain from asking you for the explanation which is due me.

Ghent bows in silence.

But there is one thing which I think I am at liberty to question.

GHENT.

Do so.

PHILIP.

I hear of your interest in a valuable mine. I hear of plans for an elaborate house. Why, then, is my sister compelled to peddle her own handiwork in a public caravansery?

GHENT.

What do you mean? I don't understand you.

PHILIP.

Points at the loom.

Her rugs and baskets are on sale in the corridor of the hotel, fingered and discussed by the tourist mob.

GHENT.

Astonished.

This can't be true!

PHILIP.

It is, however.

GHENT.

I know nothing of it. I 've had to be away a great deal. I knew she worked too hard over these things, but I took it for a mere pastime. Perhaps — No, I can't understand it at all!

PHILIP.

I advise you to make inquiries. She has taken pains to conceal her identity, but it is known nevertheless, and the subject of public curiosity.

Polly and Ruth come out from the cabin.

POLLY.

To Philip.

Take me away quickly, or I shall never enjoy upholstery again!

To Ruth.

Please change your mind, dear, and come with us for the night.

RUTH.

No. I will see you in the morning.

WINTHROP.

We leave by the early stage.

RUTH.

Looking at him quickly.

You too?

WINTHROP.

Yes, I have decided so.

RUTH.

I will be there in good time, trust me.

She kisses Polly and Philip.

Good-bye, till morning.

Gives her hand to Winthrop.

Good-bye.

Philip ignores Ghent pointedly in the leave-takings. Polly bids him farewell with corresponding cordiality.

POLLY.

Good-bye, Mr. Ghent.

*As they descend the cañon path, she is heard chatting
  enthusiastically.*

O Phil, you ought to have seen the inside of that
delightful little house!

*Her voice is heard for some time, indistinctly. Ruth, at
  the top of the path, waves to them as they descend.*

GHENT.

Looks long at her, with deep gratitude.

God bless you!

*She sits down on the rocks of the cabin terrace. He
  walks up and down in anxious thought. Once or
  twice he makes as if to speak. At length he stops before her.*

You must go in and lie down. You are worn out.

RUTH.

Rousing herself.

No, there is something I must tell you first.

GHENT.

Points at the rug.

It's about this — work you have been doing?

RUTH.

Slightly startled.

You know of that?

GHENT.

Your brother told me. I should have found it out to-morrow anyhow.

Pause.

Have you wanted money?

RUTH.

Yes.

GHENT.

I thought I — I thought you had enough. I have often begged you to take more.

RUTH.

I have n't spent what you gave me. It is in there.

She points toward the house.

GHENT.

Astonished.

You have n't spent — any of it?

RUTH.

A little. Nothing for myself.

GHENT.

But there has been no need to save, not after the first month or two. You surely knew that!

RUTH.

Yes, I knew it. It was not economy.

GHENT.

Slowly.

You have n't been willing to take money from me?

RUTH.

No. I know it was small of me, but I could n't help it. I have paid for everything. — I have kept account of it — O, to the last dreadful penny! These clothes are the ones I wore from my brother's house that night. This shelter — you know I helped to raise that with my own hands. And — and some things I paid for secretly, from the little hoard I brought away with me. You were careless; you did not notice.

GHENT.

Sits down, dizzy from the shock of her words.

I must try to grasp this!

*There is a silence, during which he sits perfectly mo-
    tionless. At last he turns to her.*

Why — why did you stand up so plucky, so
splendid, just now? Put a good face on everything about our life? Call me by my first name
and all that — before your own people?

RUTH.

We are man and wife. Beside that, my own people are as strangers.

GHENT.

Eagerly.

You say that? You can still say that?

RUTH.

Looks up, startled.

Can't you?

She awaits his answer tensely.

GHENT.

Desperately.

O, I don't know. I can't say or think anything,
after what you have just told me!

RUTH.

Wails.

You can't say it! And it is n't true! It is we who
are strangers. — Worse, a thousand times worse!

GHENT.

Rises and stands over her.

Don't let us dash ourselves to hell in one crazy
minute!

*He pauses and hesitates. When he speaks again it is
with wistful tenderness.*

Ruth, do you remember our journey here?

*She lifts her head, looking at him with white, thirsty
face.*

I thought — it seemed to me you had — begun
to care for me.

RUTH.

That night, when we rode away from the justice's
office at San Jacinto, and the sky began to
brighten over the desert — the ice that had gathered here — (*she touches her heart*) — began to melt
in spite of me. And when the next night and the
next day passed, and the next, and still you
spared me and treated me with beautiful rough

chivalry, I said to myself, "He has heard my prayer to him. He knows what a girl's heart is." As you rode before me down the arroyos, and up over the mesas, through the dazzling sunlight and the majestic silence, it seemed as if you were leading me out of a world of little codes and customs into a great new world. — So it was for those first days. — And then — and then — I woke, and saw you standing in my tent-door in the starlight! I knew before you spoke that we were lost. You had n't had the strength to save us!

GHENT.

Huskily.

Surely it has n't all been — hateful to you? There have been times, since that. — The afternoon we climbed up here. The day we made the table; the day we planted the vines.

RUTH.

In a half whisper.

Yes! — Beautiful days!

She puts her hands suddenly before her face and sobs.

O, it was not my fault! I have struggled against it. You don't know how I have struggled!

GHENT.

Against what? Struggled against what?

RUTH.

Against the hateful image you had raised up beside your own image.

GHENT.

What do you mean?

RUTH.

I mean that sometimes — often — when you stand there before my eyes, you fade away, and in your place I see — the Other One!

GHENT.

Speak plainly, for God's sake! I don't understand this talk.

RUTH.

Looking steadfastly, as at an invisible shape, speaks in a horrified whisper.

There he stands behind you now! — The human beast, that goes to its horrible pleasure as not even a wild animal will go — *in pack, in pack!*

Ghent, stung beyond endurance, rises and paces up and down. Ruth continues in a broken tone, spent by the violence of her own words.

I have tried — O, you don't know how I have tried to save myself from these thoughts. — While we were poor and struggling I thought I could do it. — Then — (*she points toward the cañon*) — then that hole down there began belching its stream of gold. You began to load me with gifts — to force easy ways upon me —

GHENT.

Well, what else did I care to make money for?

Ruth does not answer for a moment, then speaks slowly, taking the words with loathing upon her tongue.

RUTH.

Every time you give me anything, or talk about the mine and what it is going to do, there rings in my ears that dreadful sneer: "A dirt-eating Mojave would pay more than that for his squaw!"

She rises, lifting her arms.

I held myself so dear! And you bought me for a handful of gold, like a woman of the street!

You drove me before you like an animal from the market!

Ghent has seated himself again, elbows on knees and face in his hands. Ruth takes slowly from her bosom the nugget chain and holds it crumpled up in her palm. Her tone is quiet, almost matter-of-fact.

I have got back the chain again.

GHENT.

Looks up.

Chain? — What chain?

RUTH.

In the same tone, as she holds it up, letting it unwind.

The one you bought me with.

GHENT.

Dumfounded.

Where the devil —? Has that fellow been around here?

RUTH.

It would have had no meaning for me except from his hand.

GHENT.

So that 's what you 've been doing with this rug-weaving and basket-making tomfoolery?

Ruth does not answer, but continues looking at the chain, running it through her fingers and weighing it in her hand.

How long has this been going on?

RUTH.

How long? — How long can one live without breathing? Two minutes? A few lifetimes? How long!

GHENT.

It was about a month after we came here that you began to potter with this work.

RUTH.

Draws her hand about her neck as if loosening something there; convulsively.

Since then this has been round my neck, around my limbs, a chain of eating fire. Link by link I have unwound it. You will never know what it has cost me, but I have paid it all. Take it and let me go free.

She tries to force it upon him, with wailing entreaty.

Take it, take it, I beseech you!

GHENT.

Holding himself under stern control.

You are killing yourself. You must n't go on this way. Go and rest. We will talk of this to-morrow.

RUTH.

Rest! To-morrow! O, how little you have understood of all I have said! I know it is only a symbol — a make-believe. I know I am childish to ask it. Still, take it and tell me I am free.

Ghent takes the chain reluctantly, stands for a moment looking at it, then speaks with iron firmness.

GHENT.

As you say, your price has risen. This is not enough.

He throws the chain about her neck and draws her to him by it.

You are mine, mine, do you hear? Now and forever!

He starts toward the house. She holds out her hand blindly to detain him.

RUTH.

In a stifled voice.

Wait! There is — something else.

He returns to her, anxiously, and stands waiting. She goes on, touching the chain.

It is n't only for my sake I ask you to take this off me, nor only for your sake. There is — another life — to think of.

GHENT.

Leaning to look into her averted face.

Ruth! — Is it true? — Thank God!

RUTH.

Now will you take this off me?

GHENT.

Starts to do so, then draws back.

No. Now less than ever. For now, more than ever, you are mine.

RUTH.

But — *how* yours? O, remember, have pity! *How* yours?

Philip appears at the head of the cañon path. Hearing their voices, he waits, half concealed.

GHENT.

No matter how! Bought if you like, but mine!

Mine by blind chance and the hell in a man's veins, if you like! Mine by almighty Nature whether you like it or not!

RUTH.

Nature! Almighty Nature!

She takes the chain slowly from her neck.

Not yours! By everything my people have held sacred!

She drops the chain.

Not yours! Not yours!

She turns slowly. Philip has come forward, and supports her as she sinks half fainting upon his neck.

PHILIP.

To Ghent.

I came back to get my sister for the night. — I don't know by what ugly spell you have held her, but I know, from her own lips, that it is broken.

To Ruth.

Come! I have horses below.

GHENT.

No!

PHILIP.

Measuring him.

Yes.

Pause.

GHENT.

Let her say!

RUTH.

Looks long at Ghent, then at the house and surroundings. At last she turns to her brother.

Take me — with you. Take me — home!

Philip, supporting her, leads her down the cañon path. Ghent stands gazing after them as they disappear below the rim. He picks up the chain and goes back, looking down after the descending figures. The sunset light has faded, and darkness has begun to settle over the mountain world.

CURTAIN

ACT III

ACT III

Sitting-room of Mrs. Jordan's house at Milford Corners, Massachusetts. An old-fashioned New England interior, faded but showing signs of former distinction. The walls are hung with family portraits, several in clerical attire of the eighteenth century, one in the uniform of the Revolutionary War. Doors open right and left. At the back is a fireplace, flanked by windows, the curtains of which are drawn. On the left is a small table, with a lamp, books, and magazines; on the right, near the fireplace, a sewing-table, with lamp and sewing-basket. A bookcase and a writing-desk occupy opposite corners of the room, forward.

Winthrop and Philip stand near the desk, chatting. Polly is reading a newspaper at the table, left. Ruth sits before the grate, sewing; her face is turned away toward the fire.

PHILIP.

Offers Winthrop his cigar-case.

Have another cigar.

WINTHROP.

Well, as a celebration.

Takes one and lights it.

PHILIP.

Rather small business for the Jordan family, to be celebrating a bare escape from the poorhouse.

WINTHROP.

Where did you scare up the benevolent uncle? I never heard of him before.

PHILIP.

Nor I, scarcely. He 's always lived abroad.

Winthrop, strolling about, peeps over Polly's shoulder.

WINTHROP.

To Philip, with a scandalized gesture.

Stock reports!

PHILIP.

Her latest craze.

WINTHROP.

Last week it was Japanese Samurai.

POLLY.

Crushingly.

And next week it will be — Smart Alecks.

*The door on the left opens, and Mrs. Jordan enters, with
Dr. Newbury. During the preceding conversation
Ruth has sat sewing, paying no heed to the chatter.
Mrs. Jordan and the doctor look at her as they come
in, but she does not look up.*

MRS. JORDAN.

Sit down, Doctor, at least for a moment.

DR. NEWBURY.

Seats himself, Mrs. Jordan near him.

I can never resist such an invitation, in this
house.

MRS. JORDAN.

Dear Doctor, you've been a wonderful friend to
me and mine all these years, since poor Josiah
was taken.

DR. NEWBURY.

But just when you needed help most —

MRS. JORDAN.

I know how gladly you would have offered it, if
you could.

DR. NEWBURY.

Your brother-in-law in England was able to redeem the property?

MRS. JORDAN.

Hastily.

Yes, yes. — But what we are to do for the future, with my little capital gone —

She speaks lower.

O, that dreadful West! If my children had only stayed where they were born and bred.

She glances at Ruth, who has let her sewing fall in her lap and sits staring into the fire.

DR. NEWBURY.

Sotto voce.

Poor child!

Polly looks up from the newspaper excitedly, holding her finger at a place on the sheet.

POLLY.

I say, Phil! Win! Look here.

Philip and Winthrop, who have been chatting and smoking apart, come to the table.

PHILIP.

What is it now?

POLLY.

Tapping on the paper.

Something about your Arizona scheme.

PHILIP.

Bending over her, reads:

" Alleghany pig-iron, 93¾, National Brick —

POLLY.

Pointing.

No, there!

PHILIP.

Arizona Cactus Fibre, 84.

He picks up the paper, astounded.

Cactus Fibre listed! Selling at 84!

He tosses the paper to Winthrop.

This is the last straw!

MRS. JORDAN.

Who has been listening anxiously.

What does it mean, Phil?

PHILIP.

Only that the people who bought our plant and patents for a song, have made a fortune out of them.

Ruth has resumed her needle-work. Winthrop offers her the paper, with his finger at the line. She takes it, looks at it vaguely, and lays it on the table.

POLLY.

Leaning across.

Does n't that interest you?

RUTH.

Tonelessly.

O, yes.

She rises, lays her work aside, and goes toward the door, left.

DR. NEWBURY.

As she passes him.

Won't you bid me good-night, my child?

RUTH.

Giving him her hand.

Good-night, Doctor.

Dr. Newbury.

Shaking his finger.

Remember, no more moping! And from to-morrow, outdoors with you

Ruth looks at him vacantly, attempting to smile. She moves toward the door, which Winthrop opens for her.

Winthrop.

Holding out his hand.

You must bid me good-night, too, and good-bye.

Ruth.

With a faint kindling of interest.

Are you going away?

Winthrop.

Only back to Boston. Some time, when you are stronger, you will come down and see our new sailors' hospital.

Ruth.

Yes. — Good-bye.

She goes out, Winthrop closing the door.

WINTHROP.

To Dr. Newbury.

I must be going along, father. Good-night, everybody!

Patting Philip's shoulder.

Hard luck, old man!

He goes out by the hall door on the right, Philip accompanying him.

DR. NEWBURY.

Looking after his son.

Brave boy! Brave boy! He keeps up a good show.

MRS. JORDAN.

You think he still grieves over her?

DR. NEWBURY.

Ah, poor chap! He's made of the right stuff, if he is mine.

MRS. JORDAN.

Let us not talk of it. It is too sad, too dreadful.

Philip reënters.

Dr. Newbury.

About part of it we must talk.

He speaks so as to include Philip and Polly in the conversation.

Mrs. Jordan, I don't want to alarm you, but your daughter — I may as well put it bluntly — is in a dangerous state.

Mrs. Jordan.

Frightened.

Doctor! I thought she seemed so much stronger.

Dr. Newbury.

She is, so far as her body is concerned.

Mrs. Jordan sits in an attitude of nervous attention, gazing at the doctor as if trying to formulate one of many questions pressing upon her. Philip comes forward and sits by the table, near them.

Philip.

Don't you think that the routine of life which she has taken up will soon restore her to a normal state of mind?

Dr. Newbury.

Perhaps. — I hope so. — I would have good hope

of it, if it were not for her attitude toward her child.

MRS. JORDAN.

Overwhelmed.

You have noticed that, too! I have n't spoken to you of it, because — I have n't been willing to see it myself.

PHILIP.

I can't see that there is anything particularly strange in her attitude. She takes care of the brat scrupulously enough.

POLLY.

Brat!

MRS. JORDAN.

Brat!

To Dr. Newbury, after a reproachful gaze at Philip.

With the most watchful, the minutest care, but — (*she speaks in a constrained voice, with a nervous glance at the door*) — exactly as if it were a piece of machinery! — Phil, do please lay down that paper-knife before you break it! Your father brought that to me from India.

He obeys, but picks it up again absent-mindedly, after a few seconds.

Pardon me, Doctor. She goes about her daily business, and answers when she is spoken to, but as for her really being here —

She breaks out.

Doctor, what *shall* we do?

DR. NEWBURY.

She must be roused from this state, but how to do it, I don't know.

POLLY.

Rising, with heightened color and nervous emphasis.

Well, I do!

MRS. JORDAN.

Looking at her with frightened interrogation.

Polly —?

POLLY.

What she needs is her husband, and I have sent for him!

PHILIP.

Inarticulate with surprise and anger.

You —!

POLLY.

Yes, I. He's been here a week. And he's an angel, is n't he, mother?

Philip snaps the paper-knife in two, flings the pieces to the floor, and rises, pale with rage.

MRS. JORDAN.

Gathering up the pieces with a wail.

O Phil! How could you! One of my most precious relics!

PHILIP.

To Mrs. Jordan.

Is this true, or is it another of her tedious jokes?

POLLY.

Protesting.

O, my dear, tedious!

MRS. JORDAN.

Wipes her eyes, after ruefully fitting the broken pieces of the knife together and laying them tenderly on the table.

You don't deserve to have me answer you, but it is true.

PHILIP.

Was this action taken with your knowledge?

MRS. JORDAN.

I do not expect to be spoken to in that tone. Polly telegraphed merely the facts. He came at his own instance.

PHILIP.

But you have consented to enter into relations with him?

MRS. JORDAN.

I have seen him several times.

POLLY.

Triumphantly.

And yesterday we showed him the baby! Such fun, was n't it, mother?

MRS. JORDAN.

Wiping her eyes, sheepishly.

Yes, it was rather — enjoyable.

PHILIP.

He can't be in this town. I should have heard of it.

POLLY.

We 've hid him safe.

PHILIP.

Where?

POLLY.

Never mind. He's on tap, and the sooner we turn on the spigot the better, is what I think. Doctor, what do you think?

DR. NEWBURY.

Let me ask you again to state your view of Ruth's case. I don't think I quite grasp your view.

POLLY.

Pluming herself, doctrinaire.

Well! Here on the one hand is the primitive, the barbaric woman, falling in love with a romantic stranger, who, like some old Viking on a harry, cuts her with his two-handed sword from the circle of her kinsmen, and bears her away on his dragon ship toward the midnight sun. Here on the other hand is the derived, the civilized woman, with a civilized nervous system, observing that the creature eats bacon with his bowie knife, knows not the manicure, has the conversation of a preoccupied walrus, the instincts of a jealous caribou, and the endearments of a dancing crab in the mating season.

Mrs. Jordan.

Polly! What ideas! What language!

Dr. Newbury.

Don't be alarmed, Mrs. Jordan. The vocabulary has changed since our day, and — the point of view has shifted a little.

To Polly.

Well?

Polly.

Well, Ruth is one of those people who can't live in a state of divided feeling. She sits staring at this cleavage in her life, like — like that man in Dante, don't you know, who is pierced by the serpent, and who stands there in hell staring at his wound, yawning like a sleepy man.

Mrs. Jordan.

O, Polly, do please try not to get our heads muddled up with literature!

POLLY.

All I mean is that when she married her man she married him for keeps. And he did the same by her.

Philip rises, with uncontrollable impatience, and goes back to the mantelpiece, against which he leans, nervously tearing a bit of paper to pieces.

DR. NEWBURY.

Don't you think that a mere difference of cultivation, polish — or — or something of that sort — is rather small to have led to a rupture, and so painful a one too?

POLLY.

A little nonplussed.

Well, yes, perhaps it does *look* small. But we don't know the particulars; and men *are* such *colossal* brutes, you know, dear Doctor!

DR. NEWBURY.

Judicially.

Yes, so they are, so they are!

POLLY.

And then her pride! You know when it comes

to pride, Ruth would make Lucifer look like a charity-boy asking for more soup.

DR. NEWBURY.

I think perhaps the plan should be tried.

After a pause.

Yes, I think so decidedly.

PHILIP.

I call this a plot against her dignity and peace of mind!

DR. NEWBURY.

Rising.

Well, this conspirator must be going.

He shakes hands with Polly and Mrs. Jordan, takes his hat and stick. Philip remains plunged in angry reflection. Dr. Newbury taps Philip jestingly on the shoulder with the tip of his cane.

When you have lived as long as I have, my boy, you'll — you'll be just as old as I am!

He goes out, Polly accompanying him to the door.

Philip, disregarding his mother's conciliatory look and gesture as he passes her, goes out left. Polly stretches her arms and draws a deep breath as the door closes after him.

MRS. JORDAN.

Looking at her severely.

Pray what does that mean?

POLLY.

O, Phil is such a walking thunder-cloud, these days. It's a relief to get rid of him.

MRS. JORDAN.

Have you done what you could to make his life brighter?

POLLY.

I never had a chance. He has always been too much wrapped up in Ruth to think of me.

MRS. JORDAN.

How can you say such a thing? What do you suppose he married you for?

POLLY.

Heaven knows! What do they ever do it for? It is a most curious and savage propensity. But immensely interesting to watch.

MRS. JORDAN.

With a despairing gesture.

If you hold such heathenish views, why are you so bent on bringing those two together?

POLLY.

Soberly.

Because they represent — what Philip and I have missed.

MRS. JORDAN.

And pray what have "Philip and I" missed?

POLLY.

O, we're all right. But we're not like those two.

MRS. JORDAN.

I should hope not!

POLLY.

Even I believe that now and then a marriage is made in Heaven. This one was. They are pre-destined lovers!

MRS. JORDAN.

Mournfully, hypnotized by the evangelical note.

I pray it may be so.

She looks suspiciously at Polly.

You wretched girl! Predestined lovers and marriage made in Heaven, after all you 've just been saying about how impossible he is.

POLLY.

He is quite impossible, but he 's the kind we can't resist, any of us. He 'd only have to crook his little finger at me.

MRS. JORDAN.

Lifting her hands in despair.

What are you young women coming to!

Pause.

He seems to me a good man.

POLLY.

Delighted.

O, he 's *good!* So is a volcano between eruptions. And commonplace, too, until you happen to get a glimpse down one of the old volcanic rifts in his surface, and see — far below — underneath the cold lava-beds — fire, fire, the molten heart of a continent!

MRS. JORDAN.

I only hope you have some vague general notion of what you are talking about.

POLLY.

Amen. — And now let's consider when, where, and how we are to hale this dubious pair together.

MRS. JORDAN

One thing is sure, it must n't be here.

POLLY.

Why not?

MRS. JORDAN.

On Philip's account.

POLLY.

O, bother Philip! — Was n't that the doorbell?

MRS. JORDAN.

Yes. You had better go.

Polly goes out. After a moment she reënters, excitedly.

POLLY.

It's Mr. Ghent!

MRS. JORDAN.

Amazed.

Mr. Ghent?

*Polly nods enthusiastically. Ghent enters. He is con-
ventionally dressed, a black string tie and the
broad-brimmed hat which he carries being the only
suggestions of Western costume remaining. Mrs.
Jordan receives him in a flutter of excitement and
alarm.*

Mr. Ghent —! Surely at this hour —!

GHENT.

I beg your pardon. There was no other way.
I am going West to-night. — Can I see you
alone?

MRS. JORDAN.

Looks at Polly, who goes out, pouting.

Going West to-night?

GHENT.

Yes. Trouble at the mine.

MRS. JORDAN.

Is n't your business partner competent to attend
to it?

GHENT.

He 's competent to steal the whole outfit. In
fact, is doing it, or has done it already.

MRS. JORDAN.

Vaguely alarmed.

And — my property here? Is that involved in
the danger?

GHENT.

Certainly not.

MRS. JORDAN.

Relieved.

I have gone through such months of misery at
the thought of losing the dear old place! — If
Ruth only knew that we owe the very roof over
our heads to you —

GHENT.

Well, she is n't to know, that 's understood, is n't
it? Besides, it 's nothing to speak of. Glad if you
think it a service. She would n't.

MRS. JORDAN.

You mean —?

GHENT.

I mean that if she knew about it, she would n't stay here overnight.

MRS. JORDAN.

Sit down.

She motions him to a seat at the table; she sits near him, speaking with nervous impulsiveness.

Tell me what is the trouble between you! It has all been a dreadful mystery from the beginning!

GHENT.

Is it a mystery that a woman like your daughter —?

He stops and sinks into gloomy thought.

MRS. JORDAN.

Should have chosen you? — Pardon me, I don't mean anything unkind —

He makes a gesture of brusque exoneration.

But having chosen — and broken faith with her brother to do it —

GHENT.

Nervously.

Let's drop that!

Pause.

Mrs. Jordan, you come of the old stock. Do you believe in the devil?

MRS. JORDAN.

Perhaps not in the sense you mean.

GHENT.

Tapping his breast.

I mean the devil inside of a man — the devil in the heart!

MRS. JORDAN.

O, yes. We are all forced by our lives to believe in that.

GHENT.

Our lives!

He looks slowly round the room.

How long have you lived here?

MRS. JORDAN.

For thirty years, in this house. Before I was married I lived in the old house down the road yonder, opposite the church.

GHENT.

To himself.

Think of it!

MRS. JORDAN.

What did you say?

GHENT.

Gathers himself together.

Mrs. Jordan, I want you to promise that what I put in your hands from time to time comes to your daughter as if from another source.

MRS. JORDAN.

You are going away for good?

GHENT.

Yes.

MRS. JORDAN.

You give her up?

GHENT.

A man can't give up what is n't his.

MRS. JORDAN.

What is n't his? She is your wife.

GHENT.

No. Never has been.

MRS. JORDAN.

Terrified.

O, pitiful heavens!

GHENT.

I beg your pardon. — I was only trying to say —
I used to think that when a couple was married,
there they were, man and wife, and that was the
end of it. I used to think that when they had a
child, well, sure enough it was their child, and
all said. — And there's something in that, too.

*He stares before him, smiting the table and speaking
with low intensity.*

Damn me if there ain't something eternal in it!

He sits for a moment more in gloomy thought.

Do you think she 'll make up to the young one,
after a bit?

MRS. JORDAN.

O, surely! To think otherwise would be too
dreadful!

GHENT.

I'd give a good deal to know. — It's kind of lonesome for the little rooster, sitting out there all by himself on the world's doorstep! — I must see her for a minute before I go. — Do your best for me.

MRS. JORDAN.

I will do what I can.

GHENT.

You can put it as a matter of business. There is a matter of business I want to talk over with her, if I can get up the gumption.

MRS. JORDAN.

Had n't you better tell me what it is?

GHENT.

Well, it's about your son Philip. That little scheme he started out in my country — the Cactus Fibre industry.

MRS. JORDAN.

Yes?

GHENT.

I believe he thinks his sister's going away when she did queered his game.

MRS. JORDAN.

It was a severe blow to him in every way. She was the life and soul of his enterprise.

GHENT.

I want her to give him back the Cactus Fibre outfit, worth something more than when he dropped it.

MRS. JORDAN.

Give it back to him? She?

GHENT.

Takes papers from his pocket.

Yes. I happened to hear it was knocking around for nothing in the market, and I bought it — for the house, really. Hated to see that go to the dogs. Then I looked over the plant, and got a hustler to boom it. I thought as a matter of transfer, to cancel her debt, or what she thinks her debt —

Pause.

MRS. JORDAN.

Fingering the paper with hesitation.

Mr. Ghent, we really can't accept such a thing. Your offer is quixotic.

GHENT.

Quix — what?

MRS. JORDAN.

Quixotic, it really is.

GHENT.

Doubtfully.

I guess you're right. It depends on the way you look at it. One way it looks like a pure business proposition — so much lost, so much made good. The other way it looks, as you say, quix — um —. Anyway, there are the papers! Do what you think best with them.

He lays the papers on the table, and picks up his hat.

MRS. JORDAN.

Wait in the parlor.

He opens the hall door.

The second door on the left.

With an awkward bow to Mrs. Jordan, he partly closes

the door after him, when the inner door opens and Ruth appears. She goes to the sewing-table and picks up her sewing. Her mother, with a frightened glance at the half-open hall door, draws her back and kisses her. Ghent, unseen by Ruth, remains standing, with his hand on the door-knob.

Mrs. Jordan.

Ruth, you are a brave girl, and I will treat you like one. — Your husband is here.

Ruth.

Here? — Where?

Ghent pushes the door open, and closes it behind him. Ruth, sinking back against the opposite wall, stares at him blankly.

Mrs. Jordan.

He is leaving for the West again to-night. He has asked to see you before he goes.

Ruth covers her face with her hands, then fumbles blindly for the latch of the door. Her mother restrains her.

It is your duty to hear what he has to say. You owe that to the love you once bore him.

Ruth.

He killed my love before it was born!

MRS. JORDAN.

It is your duty to hear him, and part with him in a Christian spirit, for our sakes, if not for your own.

RUTH.

For whose sake?

MRS. JORDAN.

For mine, and your brother's. — We owe it to him, as a family.

GHENT.

Raises his hand restrainingly.

Mrs. Jordan —!

RUTH.

Owe?

MRS. JORDAN.

We owe it to him, for what he has done and wishes to do.

RUTH.

What he has done? — Wishes to do?

MRS. JORDAN.

Yes, don't echo me like a parrot! He has done a

great deal for us, and is anxious to do more, if you will only let him.

RUTH.

What is this? Explain it to me quickly.

MRS. JORDAN.

With growing impatience.

Don't think to judge your mother!

RUTH.

I demand to hear what all this is! Tell me.

MRS. JORDAN.

Losing control of herself.

He has kept us from being turned into the street!

Ghent, who has tried dumbly to restrain her, turns away in stoic resignation to his fate.

He has given us the very roof over our heads!

RUTH.

You said that uncle —

MRS. JORDAN.

Well, it was not your uncle! I said so to shield you in your stubborn and cold-hearted pride.

RUTH.

Is there more of this?

MRS. JORDAN.

Yes, there *is* more. You wronged your brother to follow your own path of wilful love, and now you wrong him again by following your own path of wilful aversion. Here comes your husband, offering to make restitution —

RUTH.

What restitution?

MRS. JORDAN.

He has bought Philip's property out there, and wants you to give it back to him.

Ruth stands motionless for a moment, then looks vacantly about, speaking in a dull voice, as at first.

RUTH.

I must go away from this house.

MRS. JORDAN.

You don't understand. He claims nothing. He is going away himself immediately. Whatever

this dreadful trouble is between you, you are his
wife, and he has a right to help you and yours.

RUTH.

I am not his wife.

MRS. JORDAN.

Ruth, don't frighten me. He said those same
words —

RUTH.

He said — what?

MRS. JORDAN.

That you were not his wife.

RUTH.

He said — that?

MRS. JORDAN.

Yes, but afterward he explained —

RUTH.

Flaming into white wrath.

Explained! Did he explain that when I was left
alone that night at the ranch he came — with

two others — and when gun and knife had failed me, and nothing stood between me and their drunken fury, I sold myself to the strongest of them, hiding my head behind the name of marriage?   Did he explain that between him and the others money clinked — (*she raps on the table*) — my price in hard money on the table? And now that I have run away to the only refuge I have on earth, he comes to buy the very house where I have hidden, and every miserable being within it!

Long pause. She looks about blankly and sinks down by the table.

MRS. JORDAN.

Cold and rigid.

And you — married him — after that?

She turns away in horror-stricken judgment.

You ought to have — died — first!

Philip opens the door and enters, staring at Ghent with dislike and menace.

O Philip, she has told me! — You can't imagine what horrors!

Ruth rises, with fright in her face, and approaches her brother to restrain him.

PHILIP.

Horrors? What horrors?

MRS. JORDAN.

It was your fault! You ought never to have left her alone in that dreadful place! She — she married him — to save herself — from — O horrible!

Philip waits an instant, the truth penetrating his mind slowly. Then, with mortal rage in his face, he starts toward Ghent.

PHILIP.

You — dog!

Ruth throws herself in Philip's path.

RUTH.

No, no, no!

PHILIP.

Get out of my way. This is my business now.

RUTH.

No, it is mine. I tell you it is mine.

PHILIP.

We 'll see whose it is. I said that if the truth ever

came out, this man should answer to me, and now, by God, he shall answer!

With another access of rage he tries to thrust Ruth from his path. Mrs. Jordan, terrified at the storm she has raised, clings desperately to her son's arm.

RUTH.

I told him long ago it should be between us. Now it shall be between us.

MRS. JORDAN.

Philip! For my sake, for your father's sake! Don't, don't! You will only make it worse. In pity's name, leave them alone together. Leave them alone — together!

They force Philip back to the door, where he stands glaring at Ghent.

PHILIP.

To Ghent.

My time will come. Meanwhile, hide behind the skirts of the woman whose life you have ruined and whose heart you have broken. Hide behind her. It is the coward's privilege. Take it.

Philip, with Mrs. Jordan still clinging to his arm, goes out, Ruth closing the door after them. She and Ghent

*confront each other in silence for a moment, across
the width of the room.*

RUTH.

God forgive me! You never can.

GHENT.

It was a pity — but — you were in a corner. I
drove you to it, by coming here.

RUTH.

It was base of me — base!

GHENT.

The way your mother took it showed me one
thing. — I 've never understood you, because —
I don't understand your people.

RUTH.

You mean — her saying I ought to have died
rather than accept life as I did?

GHENT.

Yes.

RUTH.

She spoke the truth. I have always seen it.

GHENT.

Ruth, it's a queer thing for me to be saying, but — it seems to me, you've never seen the truth between us.

RUTH.

What is the truth — between us?

GHENT.

The truth is —

He pauses, then continues with a disconsolate gesture.

Well, there's no use going into that.

He fumbles in his pocket, and takes from it the nugget chain, which he looks at in silence for a time, then speaks in quiet resignation.

I've got here the chain, that's come, one way and another, to have a meaning for us. For you it's a bitter meaning, but, all the same, I want you to keep it. Show it some day to the boy, and tell him — about me.

He lays it on the desk and goes toward the door.

RUTH.

What is the truth — between us?

GHENT.

I guess it was only of myself I was thinking.

RUTH.

What is it — about yourself?

GHENT.

After a pause.

I drifted into one of your meeting-houses last
Sunday, not knowing where else to go, and I
heard a young fellow preaching about what he
called "The Second Birth." A year and a half ago
I should have thought it was all hocus-pocus,
but you can believe me or not, the way he went
on he might have been behind the door that
night in that little justice den at San Jacinto,
saying to the Recording Angel: "Do you see that
rascal? Take notice! There ain't an ounce of
bone or a drop of blood in him but what 's new
man!"

RUTH.

You think it has been all my fault — the failure
we 've made of our life?

GHENT.

It 's been no failure. However it is, it 's been our life, and in my heart I think it 's been — all — right!

RUTH.

All right! O, how can you say that?

She repeats the words with a touch of awe and wonder.

All right!

GHENT.

Some of it has been wrong, but as a whole it has been right — right! I know that does n't happen often, but it has happened to us, because — (*he stops, unable to find words for his idea*) because — because the first time our eyes met, they burned away all that was bad in our meeting, and left only the fact that we *had* met — pure good — pure joy — a fortune of it — for both of us. Yes, for both of us! You 'll see it yourself some day.

RUTH.

If you had only heard my cry to you, to wait, to cleanse yourself and me — by suffering and sacrifice — before we dared begin to live! But

you would n't see the need! — O, if you could
have felt for yourself what I felt for you! If you
could have said, "The wages of sin is death!"
and suffered the anguish of death, and risen again
purified! But instead of that, what you had done
fell off from you like any daily trifle.

GHENT.

*Steps impulsively nearer her, sweeping his hand to
indicate the portraits on the walls.*

Ruth, it 's these fellows are fooling you! It 's they
who keep your head set on the wages of sin, and
all that rubbish. What have we got to do with
suffering and sacrifice? That may be the law for
some, and I 've tried hard to see it as our law,
and thought I had succeeded. But I have n't!
Our law is joy, and selfishness; the curve of your
shoulder and the light on your hair as you sit there
says that as plain as preaching. — Does it gall
you the way we came together? You asked me
that night what brought me, and I told you
whiskey, and sun, and the devil. Well, I tell you
now I'm thankful on my knees for all three!
Does it rankle in your mind that I took you when
I could get you, by main strength and fraud? I
guess most good women are taken that way, if

they only knew it. Don't you want to be paid for? I guess every wife is paid for in some good coin or other. And as for you, I 've paid for you not only with a trumpery chain, but with the heart in my breast, do you hear? That 's one thing you can't throw back at me — the man you 've made of me, the life and the meaning of life you 've showed me the way to!

Ruth's face is hidden in her hands, her elbows on the table. He stands over her, flushed and waiting. Gradually the light fades from his face. When he speaks again, the ring of exultation which has been in his voice is replaced by a sober intensity.

If you can't see it my way, give me another chance to live it out in yours.

He waits, but she does not speak or look up. He takes a package of letters and papers from his pocket, and runs them over, in deep reflection.

During the six months I 've been East —

RUTH.

Looking up.

Six months? Mother said a week!

GHENT.

Your sister-in-law's telegram was forwarded to

me here. I let her think it brought me, but as a matter of fact, I came East in the next train after yours. It was rather a low-lived thing to do, I suppose, hanging about and bribing your servant for news —

Ruth lets her head sink in her hands. He pauses and continues ruefully.

I might have known how that would strike you! Well, it would have come out sooner or later. — That's not what I started to talk about. — You ask me to suffer for my wrong. Since you left me I *have* suffered — God knows! You ask me to make some sacrifice. Well — how would the mine do? Since I've been away they've as good as stolen it from me. I could get it back easy enough by fighting; but supposing I don't fight. Then we'll start all over again just as we stand in our shoes, and make another fortune — for our boy.

Ruth utters a faint moan as her head sinks in her arms on the table. With trembling hands, Ghent caresses her hair lightly, and speaks between a laugh and a sob.

Little mother! Little mother! What does the past matter, when we've got the future — and him?

Ruth does not move. He remains bending over her for some moments, then straightens up, with a gesture of stoic despair.

I know what you're saying there to yourself, and I guess you're right. Wrong is wrong, from the moment it happens till the crack of doom, and all the angels in Heaven, working overtime, can't make it less or different by a hair. That seems to be the law. I've learned it hard, but I guess I've learned it. I've seen it written in mountain letters across the continent of this life. — Done is done, and lost is lost, and smashed to hell is smashed to hell. We fuss and potter and patch up. You might as well try to batter down the Rocky Mountains with a rabbit's heart-beat!

He goes to the door, where he turns.

You've fought hard for me, God bless you for it. — But it's been a losing game with you from the first! — You belong here, and I belong out yonder — beyond the Rockies, beyond — the Great Divide!

He opens the door and is about to pass out. Ruth looks up with streaming eyes.

RUTH.

Wait!

*He closes the door and stands waiting for her to speak.
Ruth masters herself and goes on, her eyes shining,
her face exalted.*

Tell me you know that if I could have followed
you, and been your wife, without struggle and
without bitterness, I would have done it.

GHENT.

Solemnly.

I believe you would.

RUTH.

Tell me you know that when I tore down with
bleeding fingers the life you were trying to
build for us, I did it only — because — I loved
you!

GHENT.

*Comes slowly to the table, looking at her with bewilder-
ment.*

How was that?

RUTH.

O, I don't wonder you ask! Another woman
would have gone straight to her goal. You might
have found such a one. But instead you found

me, a woman in whose ears rang night and day the cry of an angry Heaven to us both — "Cleanse yourselves!" And I went about doing it in the only way I knew — (*she points at the portraits on the wall*) — the only way my fathers knew — by wretchedness, by self-torture, by trying blindly to pierce your careless heart with pain. And all the while you — O, as I lay there and listened to you, I realized it for the first time — you had risen, in one hour, to a wholly new existence, which flooded the present and the future with brightness, yes, and reached back into our past, and made of it — made of all of it — something to cherish!

She takes the chain, and comes closer.

You have taken the good of our life and grown strong. I have taken the evil and grown weak, weak unto death. Teach me to live as you do!

She puts the chain about her neck.

GHENT.

Puzzled, not yet realizing the full force of her words.

Teach you — to live — as I do?

RUTH.

And teach — *him!*

GHENT.

Unable to realize his fortune.

You 'll let me help make a kind of a happy life
for — the little rooster?

RUTH.

Holds out her arms, her face flooded with happiness.

And for us! For us!

CURTAIN

THE FAITH HEALER

A Play in Three Acts

PERSONS OF THE PLAY

ULRICH MICHAELIS

MATTHEW BEELER

MARY BEELER, *his wife*

MARTHA BEELER, *his sister*

ANNIE BEELER, *his daughter*

RHODA WILLIAMS, *Mrs. Beeler's niece*

DR. GEORGE LITTLEFIELD

REV. JOHN CULPEPPER

UNCLE ABE, *an old negro*

AN INDIAN BOY

A YOUNG MOTHER WITH HER BABY

VARIOUS SICK PEOPLE AND OTHERS ATTENDANT
UPON THEM

ACT I

ACT I

A large old-fashioned room in Matthew Beeler's farm-house, near a small town in the Middle West. The room is used for dining and for general living purposes. It suggests, in architecture and furnishings, a past of considerable prosperity, which has now given place to more humble living. The house is, in fact, the ancestral home of Mr. Beeler's wife, Mary, born Beardsley, a family of the local farming aristocracy, now decayed. At the rear is a large double window, set in a broad alcove. To the right of the window is the entrance door, which opens upon the side yard, showing bushes, trees, and farm buildings.

In the right wall of the room a door and covered stairway lead to the upper story. Farther forward is a wall cupboard, and a door leading into the kitchen. Opposite this cupboard, in the left-hand wall of the room, is a mantelpiece and grate; farther back a double door, leading to a hall. Off the hall open two bedrooms (not seen), one belonging to Mr. and Mrs. Beeler, the other to Rhoda Williams, a niece of Mrs. Beeler, child of her dead sister.

The room contains, among other articles of furniture, a dining table (with detachable leaves to reduce its bulk when not in use for eating purposes), an invalid's wheel-chair, a low sofa of generous size, and a book-shelf, upon which are arranged the scientific books which Mr. Beeler takes a somewhat untutored but genuine delight in. Tacked upon the wall near by are portraits of scientific men, Darwin and Spencer conspicuous among them, cut from periodicals.

175

Other pictures, including family daguerreotypes and photographs, are variously distributed about the walls. Over the mantel shelf hangs a large map of the United States and Mexico, faded and fly-specked.

As the curtain rises, the room is dark, except for a dull fire in the grate. The ticking of the clock is heard; it strikes six. Martha Beeler, a woman of forty-five, enters from the kitchen, carrying a lighted lamp. She wears a shawl over her shoulders, a print dress, and a kitchen apron. She places the lamp on the table, which is set for breakfast, and puts coal on the grate, which soon flames more brightly. She goes into the hall and is heard knocking and calling.

MARTHA.

Rhody! Rhody!

Matthew Beeler, a man of fifty, enters. He is not quite dressed, but finishes as he comes in. Martha follows him.

Where's that niece of yours got to now?

BEELER.

She's helping Mary dress.

MARTHA.

What in time's Mary gettin' up for? She's only in the way till the work's done.

BEELER.

She's restless.

MARTHA.

Significantly.

I shouldn't wonder. *Pause.* I hope you know *why* Mary didn't sleep.

BEELER.

Evasively.

She's always been a light sleeper, since she got her stroke.

MARTHA.

Look here, Mat Beeler! I'm your born sister. Don't try to fool me! You know why your wife didn't sleep last night.

BEELER.

Maybe I do, Sis.

Points to the ceiling.

Is he up yet?

MARTHA.

Up! I don't believe he's been abed.

They listen, as to the tread of some one on the floor above.

Back and forth, like a tiger in a cage!

BEELER.

Shrugs.

Queer customer.

MARTHA.

Yes.

Imitates him.

" Queer customer," that's you.   But come to doin' anything about it !

BEELER.

Give me time, Sis, give me time !

MARTHA.

How much time do you want ?   He's been in this house since Wednesday night, and this is Saturday morning.

BEELER.

Well, he's payin' his board, ain't he ?

At window, rolls up curtain.

Goin' to have just such another day as yesterday. Never seen such a fog.

MARTHA.

Never seen such a fog, eh ?

Comes nearer and speaks mysteriously.

Did you happen to notice how long that fog has been hangin' over this house ?

BEELER.

How long?   Why, since Thursday.

MARTHA.

No, sir, since Wednesday night.

BEELER.

Looking at her, astonished.

Martha Beeler!   You don't mean to say — he *brought* the fog?

She flounces out without answering.   He lights lantern, with dubious head-shaking, and holds it up before the print portraits.

Mornin', Mr. Darwin.   Same to you, Mr. Spencer.   Still keepin' things straight?

Grunts as he turns down his lantern, which is smoking.

I guess not very.

The hall door again opens, and Rhoda Williams, a girl of twenty, enters, with Annie Beeler, a child of ten.   Rhoda is running, with Annie in laughing pursuit.

RHODA.

Taking refuge behind the table.

King's X!

ANNIE.

Catching her.

You didn't have your fingers crossed.

RHODA.

*Turning Annie about, and beginning to button the child's
long slip.*

And you didn't have your dress buttoned.

ANNIE.

That doesn't count.

RHODA.

Yes, it does, before breakfast!

BEELER.

At the outer door.

How does your aunt strike you this morning?

RHODA.

Sobered.

She seems wonderfully better.

BEELER.

Better!

RHODA.

I don't mean her poor body. She's got past
caring for that.

BEELER.

With sarcasm.

You mean in her mind, eh?

RHODA.

Yes, I mean better in her mind.

BEELER.

Because of what this fellow has been sayin' to her, I suppose.

RHODA.

Yes, because of that.

BEELER.

As he puts on an old fur cap.

An out-and-out fakir!

RHODA.

You don't know him.

BEELER.

I suppose you do, after forty-eight hours. What in the name of nonsense is he, anyway? And this deaf and dumb Indian boy he drags around with him. What's his part in the show?

RHODA.

I know very little about either of them.   But I know Mr. Michaelis is not — what you say.

BEELER.

Well, he's a crank at the best of it.   He's worked your aunt up now so's she can't sleep.   You brought him here, and you've got to get rid of him.

Exit by outer door, with inarticulate grumblings, among which can be distinguished.

Hump! Ulrich Michaelis! There's a name for you.

ANNIE.

What's a fakir?

Rhoda does not answer.

Cousin Rho, what's a fakir?

RHODA.

Humoring her.

A man, way off on the other side of the world, in India, who does strange things.

ANNIE.

What kind of things?

RHODA.

Well, for instance, he throws a rope up in the air, right up in the empty air, with nothing for it to catch on, and then — he — climbs — up — the — rope!

ANNIE.

Don't he fall?

Rhoda shakes her head in portentous negation.
Steps are heard descending the stairs. The child fidgets
nervously.

ANNIE.

Listen! He's coming down!

RHODA.

Yes, he's coming down, right out of the blue sky.

ANNIE.

In a panic.

Let me go.

She breaks away and retreats to the hall door, watching the
stair door open, and Ulrich Michaelis enter. Thereupon,
with a glance of frightened curiosity, she flees. Michaelis
is a man of twenty-eight or thirty, and his dark, emaciated
face, wrinkled by sun and wind, looks older. His abundant
hair is worn longer than common. His frame, though
slight, is powerful, and his way of handling himself has the
freedom and largeness which come from much open-air life.
There is nevertheless something nervous and restless in his
movements. He has a trick of handling things, putting
them down only to take them up again immediately, before
renouncing them for good. His face shows the effect of
sleeplessness, and his gray flannel shirt and dark, coarse
clothing are rumpled and neglected.

RHODA.

As he enters.

Good morning.

MICHAELIS.

Watching Annie's retreat.

Is — is that child afraid of me?

RHODA.

As she adds the finishing touches to the breakfast table.

Oh, Annie's a queer little body. She has her mother's nerves. And then she sees no one, living here on the back road. If this dreadful fog ever lifts, you'll see that, though we're quite near town, it's almost as if we were in the wilderness.

The stair door opens, and an Indian boy, about sixteen years old, enters. He is dressed in ordinary clothes; his dark skin, longish hair, and the noiseless tread of his moccasined feet, are the only suggestions of his race. He bows to Rhoda, who returns his salutation; then, with a glance at Michaelis, he goes out doors.

Rhoda nods toward the closing door.

It's really him Annie's afraid of. He's like a creature from another world, to her.

MICHAELIS.

Looks at her in an odd, startled way.

Another world?

RHODA.

Oh, you're used to his people.   Your father was a missionary to the Indians, you told me.

MICHAELIS.

Yes.

RHODA.

Where?

MICHAELIS.

At Acoma.

RHODA.

Where is that?

MICHAELIS.

Standing near the wall map, touches it.

In New Mexico, by the map.

RHODA.

Comes nearer.

What is it like?

MICHAELIS.

It's — as you say — another world.

RHODA.

Describe it to me.

MICHAELIS.

I couldn't make you see it. It's — centuries and centuries from our time. — And since I came here, since I entered this house, it has seemed centuries away from my own life.

RHODA.

My life has seemed far off, too — my old life —

MICHAELIS.

What do you mean by your old life?

RHODA.

She breaks out impulsively.

I mean — I mean —.   Three days ago I was like one dead!   I walked and ate and did my daily tasks, but — I wondered sometimes why people didn't see that I was dead, and scream at me.

MICHAELIS.

It was three days ago that I first saw you.

RHODA.

Yes.

MICHAELIS.

Three nights ago, out there in the moonlit country.

RHODA.

Yes.

MICHAELIS.

You were unhappy, then?

RHODA.

The dead are not unhappy, and I was as one dead.

MICHAELIS.

Why was that?

RHODA.

I think we die more than once when things are too hard and too bitter.

MICHAELIS.

Have things here been hard and bitter?

RHODA.

No.   All that was before I came here!   But it had left me feeling —.   The other night, as I walked through the streets of the town, the people seemed like ghosts to me, and I myself like a ghost.

MICHAELIS.

I cannot think of you as anything but glad and free.

RHODA.

When you met me on the road, and walked home with me, and said those few words, it was as if, all of a sudden, the dead dream was shattered, and I began once more to live.

Bell rings.

That is Aunt Mary's bell.

Rhoda goes out by the hall door, wheeling the invalid chair. Martha enters from the kitchen, carrying a steaming coffee-pot and a platter of smoking meat, which she places on the table.   Michaelis bows to her.

MARTHA.

Snappishly.

Hope you slept well!

She goes to the outer door, rings the breakfast bell loudly, and exit to kitchen.   Rhoda enters, wheeling Mrs. Beeler in an invalid chair.   Mrs. Beeler is a woman of forty, slight of body, with hair just beginning to silver.   Her face has the curious refinement which physical suffering sometimes brings.   Annie lingers at the door, looking timidly at Michaelis, as he approaches Mrs. Beeler and takes her hand from the arm of the chair.

MICHAELIS.

You are better?

MRS. BEELER.

Speaks with low intensity.

Much, much better.

He puts her hand gently back on the chair arm. Martha enters with other dishes. She pours out coffee, putting a cup at each plate. Mr. Beeler has entered from the kitchen, and the boy from outside. Beeler, with a glance of annoyance at his wife and Michaelis, sits down at the head of the table. Rhoda pushes Mrs. Beeler's chair to the foot of the table and stands feeding her, eating her own breakfast meanwhile.

Michaelis sits at Mrs. Beeler's right, Martha opposite. At Mr. Beeler's right is the Indian boy, at his left Annie's vacant chair. Martha beckons to Annie to come to the table, but the child, eyeing the strangers, refuses, taking a chair behind her mother by the mantelpiece. Mrs. Beeler speaks after the meal has progressed for some time in silence.

MRS. BEELER.

Mat, you haven't said good morning to our guest.

BEELER.

Gruffly.

How are you?

He helps himself to meat and passes it to the others; the plate goes round the table. There is a constrained silence.

Annie tugs at Rhoda's skirt, and asks in dumb show to have her breakfast given her. Rhoda fills the child's plate, with which she retreats to her place by the mantel.

MRS. BEELER.

Why doesn't Annie come to the table?

She tries to look around. Rhoda whispers to Mrs. Beeler, who looks at her, puzzled.

Why doesn't Annie come?

RHODA.

She's afraid.

MRS. BEELER.

Afraid! What is she afraid of?

RHODA.

You know how shy she is, before strangers.

MRS. BEELER.

Annie, please come here! Annie!

The child refuses, pouting, and gazing at Michaelis.

RHODA.

I wouldn't urge her. She doesn't want to come.

MARTHA.

Trenchantly.

Don't blame her!

MRS. BEELER.

Gently reproving.

Martha!

MICHAELIS.

Holding out his hand to Annie.

Won't you come here, my child?

Annie approaches slowly, as if hypnotized.

You're not afraid of me, are you?

ANNIE.

Shyly.

Not if you won't climb up the rope.

MICHAELIS.

Puzzled.

Climb up what rope?

RHODA.

It's a story I was foolish enough to tell her.
— Do eat something, Auntie.

MRS. BEELER.

I'll drink a little more tea.

Rhoda raises the cup to Mrs. Beeler's lips.

BEELER.

You can't live on tea, Mary.

MARTHA.

I guess she can live on tea better than on some things!

With a resentful glance at Michaelis.

Some things that some folks seem to live on, and expect other folks to live on.

Michaelis looks up from Annie, who has been whispering in his ear. Beeler nods at Martha in covert approval, as she takes up dishes and goes into the kitchen.

MRS. BEELER.

Leans forward across the table to Michaelis.

Don't mind my sister-in-law, Mr. Michaelis. It's her way.   She means nothing by it.

BEELER.

Between gulps of coffee, as he finishes his meal.

Don't know as you've got any call to speak for Martha.   She generally means what she says, and I guess she means it now.   And what's more, I guess I do, too!

MRS. BEELER.

Beseechingly.

Mat!

BEELER.

Throws down his napkin and rises.

Very well.   It's none of my business, I reckon, as long as it keeps within reason.

He puts on his cap and goes out through the kitchen.

ANNIE.

To Michaelis, continuing the whispered conversation.

And if you do climb up the rope, do you promise to come down.

MICHAELIS.

Yes, I promise to come down.

MRS. BEELER.

Leans over her plate.   The others bow their heads.

Bless this food to our use, and this day to our strength and our salvation.

RHODA.

As they lift their heads.

Perhaps it will be light enough now without the lamp.

Michaelis, holding Annie's hand, rises, goes to the window, and rolls up the shades, while Rhoda extinguishes the lamp. The fog is still thick, and the light which enters is dull.

Rhoda unpins the napkin from her aunt's breast, and wheels her back from the table. The boy crouches down by the grate, Indian fashion. Annie looks at him with shy, half-frightened interest.

MRS. BEELER.

Gazing out, from where she sits reclining.

The blessed sun! I never thought to see it rise again so beautiful.

RHODA.

Looks at her aunt, puzzled and alarmed.

But, Auntie, there isn't any sun! It's —

She breaks off, seeing Michaelis place his finger on his lips as a signal for her to be silent. Mrs. Beeler turns to Rhoda, puzzled.

MRS. BEELER.

There isn't any sun? Why —

Rhoda pretends not to hear. Mrs. Beeler turns to Michaelis.

What does she mean by saying there is no sun?

MICHAELIS.

She means she doesn't see it.

MRS. BEELER.

Still puzzled.

But — you see it, don't you?

MICHAELIS.

I see the same sun that you see.

MRS. BEELER.

Looks again at Rhoda, then dismisses her wonderment, and looks out at the window dreamily.

Another day — and to-morrow the best of all the days of the year.

ANNIE.

What day is to-morrow?

She leaves Michaelis and comes to her mother's side.

What day is to-morrow?

MRS. BEELER.

With exultation in her voice.

My child, to-morrow is the most wonderful and the most beautiful day of all the year. The day when — all over the whole world — there is singing in the air, and everything rises into new life and happiness.

ANNIE.

Fretfully.

Mamma, I don't understand! What day is to-morrow?

MRS. BEELER.

To-morrow is Easter.

ANNIE.

With sudden interest.

Easter!   Can I have some eggs to color?

MRS. BEELER.

Ask Aunt Martha.

ANNIE.

Singsong, as she skips out.

Eggs to color!   Eggs to color!

Rhoda has meanwhile fetched a large tray from the cupboard and has been piling the dishes noiselessly upon it.

RHODA.

Shall I wheel you in, Aunt Mary?

MRS. BEELER.

Yes, please.

Rhoda wheels the chair toward the hall door, which Michaelis opens.   Mrs. Beeler gazes at him as she passes.

Will you come in soon, and sit with me?   There is so much that I want to hear.

MICHAELIS.

Whenever you are ready.

Mrs. Beeler.

I will ring my bell.

As they go out, Martha bustles in, gathers up the dish tray and is about to depart, with a vindictive look. At the door she turns, and jerks her head toward the boy.

Martha.

Is it against the law to work where he comes from?

Michaelis.

Abstractedly.

What? — No.

Martha.

Then he might as well do me some chores. Not but right, payin' only half board.

Michaelis.

To the boy.

Do whatever she tells you.

The boy follows Martha out. Michaelis stands by the window in thought. As Rhoda reënters, he looks up. He speaks significantly, with suppressed excitement.

She saw the sun!

Rhoda.

Poor dear Auntie!

MICHAELIS.

You pity her?

RHODA.

After an instant's silence, during which she ponders her reply.

I think I envy her.

She removes the cloth from the table, and begins deftly to put the room in order. Michaelis watches her with a kind of vague intentness.

MICHAELIS.

How long did you say she had been sick?

RHODA.

More than four years — nearly five.

MICHAELIS.

She has never walked in that time?

RHODA.

Shakes her head.

Nor used her right hand, either.

MICHAELIS.

With intensity.

Are you certain?

RHODA.

Surprised at his tone.

Yes — I haven't lived here long, but I am certain.

MICHAELIS.

She has tried medicine, doctors?

RHODA.

Uncle has spent everything he could earn on
them.   She has been three times to the min-
eral baths, once as far as Virginia.

MICHAELIS.

But never as far as Bethesda.

RHODA.

Bethesda?   Where is that?

MICHAELIS.

The pool, which is called Bethesda, having five
porches.

RHODA.

Oh, yes.   The pool in the Bible, where once a
year an angel troubled the waters, and the sick
and the lame and the blind gathered, hoping to
be healed.

MICHAELIS.

And whoever first, after the troubling of the
waters, stepped in, he was made whole of what-
soever disease he had.

RHODA.

If anybody could find the way there again, it would be Aunt Mary.

Pause.

And if anybody could show her the way it would be — you.

She goes on in a different tone, as if to escape from the embarrassment of her last speech.

Her saying just now she saw the sun. She often says things like that. Have you noticed?

MICHAELIS.

Yes.

RHODA.

With hesitation.

Her brother Seth — the one who died — has she told you about him?

MICHAELIS.

Yes.

RHODA.

What she thinks happens — since — he died?

Michaelis nods assent.

And yet in most other ways her mind is perfectly clear.

MICHAELIS.

Perhaps in this way it is clearer still.

RHODA.

Startled.

You mean — that maybe she really does — *see* her brother?

MICHAELIS.

It may be.

RHODA.

It would make the world a very different — a very strange place, if that *were* true.

MICHAELIS.

The world *is* a very strange place.

Pause.

RHODA.

Tell me a little about your life.   That seems to have been very strange.

MICHAELIS.

Vaguely, as he seats himself by the table.

I don't know. I can hardly remember what my life was.

RHODA.

Why is that?

MICHAELIS.

Gazing at her.

Because, since I came into this house, I have seen the vision of another life.

RHODA.

With hesitation.

What — other life?

MICHAELIS.

Since my boyhood I have been —

He hesitates.

I have been a wanderer, almost a fugitive —. And I never knew it, till now — I never knew it till — I looked into your face!

RHODA.

Avoiding his gaze.

How should that make you know?

MICHAELIS.

Leans nearer.

All my life long I have walked in the light of something to come, some labor, some mission, I

have scarcely known what — but I have risen
with it and lain down with it, and nothing else
has existed for me. — Nothing, until — I lifted
my eyes and you stood there.   The stars looked
down from their places, the earth wheeled on
among the stars.   Everything was as it had
been, and nothing was as it had been; nor ever,
ever can it be the same again.

Rhoda.

In a low and agitated voice.

You must not say these things to me.   You are —
I am not —.   You must not think of me so.

Michaelis.

I must think of you as I must.

*Pause.   Rhoda speaks in a lighter tone, as if to relieve the
tension of their last words.*

Rhoda.

Tell me a little of your boyhood. — What was
it like — that place where you lived?

Michaelis.

Becomes absorbed in his own mental pictures as he speaks.

A great table of stone, rising five hundred feet
out of the endless waste of sand.   A little

adobe house, halfway up the mesa, with the desert far below and the Indian village far above. A few peach trees, and a spring — a sacred spring, which the Indians worshipped in secret. A little chapel, which my father had built with his own hands.   He often spent the night there, praying.   And there, one night, he died. I found him in the morning, lying as if in quiet prayer before the altar.

RHODA.

After a moment's hush.

What did you do after your father died?

MICHAELIS.

I went away south, into the mountains, and got work on a sheep range.   I was a shepherd for five years.

RHODA.

And since then?

MICHAELIS.

Hesitates.

Since then I have — wandered about, working here and there to earn enough to live on.

RHODA.

I understand well why men take up that life.
I should love it myself.

MICHAELIS.

I didn't do it because I loved it.

RHODA.

Why, then?

MICHAELIS.

I was waiting my time.

RHODA.

In a low tone.

Your time — for what?

MICHAELIS.

To fulfil my life — my real life.

RHODA.

Your — real life?

*He sits absorbed in thought without answering. Rhoda
continues, after a long pause.*

There in the mountains, when you were a shepherd — that was not your real life?

MICHAELIS.

It was the beginning of it.

RHODA.

With hesitation.

Won't you tell me a little about that time?

MICHAELIS.

In the fall I would drive the sheep south, through the great basin which sloped down into Mexico, and in the spring back again to the mountains.

RHODA.

Were you all alone?

MICHAELIS.

There were a few men on the ranges, but they were no more to me than the sheep — not so much.

RHODA.

Weren't you dreadfully lonely?

MICHAELIS.

No.

RHODA.

You hadn't even any books to read?

MICHAELIS.

Takes a book from his coat pocket.

I had this pocket Bible, that had been my father's. I read that sometimes. But always in a dream, without understanding, without remembering.

His excitement increases.

Yet there came a time when whole chapters started up in my mind, as plain as if the printed page were before me, and I understood it all, both the outer meaning and the inner.

RHODA.

And you didn't know what made the difference?

MICHAELIS.

Yes.

RHODA.

What was it?

MICHAELIS.

I can't tell you that.

RHODA.

Oh, yes!

MICHAELIS.

There are no words to tell of it.

RHODA.

Yet tell me. I need to know. Believe me, I need to know!

MICHAELIS.

Slowly, groping for his words.

It was one morning in the fourth spring. We were back in the mountains again. It was lambing time, and I had been up all night. Just before sunrise, I sat down on a rock to rest. Then — it came.

RHODA.

What came?

He does not answer.

You saw something?

He nods for yes.

What was it?

MICHAELIS.

Rises, lifting his arms, a prey to uncontrollable excitement.

The living Christ! — Standing before me on the mountain, amid the grazing sheep. — With these eyes and in this flesh, I saw Him.

Long pause.

RHODA.

In a low tone.

You had fallen asleep. It was a dream.

MICHAELIS.

Shakes his head in negation.

That wasn't all.

He turns away. She follows him, and speaks after a silence.

RHODA.

Tell me the rest. What happened to you, after — after what you saw — that morning in the mountains?

MICHAELIS.

Begins to talk slowly and reluctantly.

I lived straight ahead, with the sheep for two years.

RHODA.

Hesitating.

Did you ever *see* anything again?

MICHAELIS.

No. — But twice — I heard a voice.

RHODA.

What kind of a voice?

MICHAELIS.

The first time it came at night. I was walking on the top of the mountain, in a stony place. It — it was like a wind among the stones.

RHODA.

What did it say?

MICHAELIS.

It said, " Prepare! Prepare!"

RHODA.

And the second time?

MICHAELIS.

In the same place, at dawn.   The voice said,
" Go forth, it is finished!"   I looked round me
and saw nothing.   Then it came again, like a
wind among the stones, " Go forth, it is begun!"

RHODA.

And you obeyed?

MICHAELIS.

I found a man to take my place, and started
north.   Three days after, I climbed the mesa
toward my old home.   Above, in the pueblo, I
heard the sound of tom-toms and wailing squaws.
They told me that the young son of the chief
lay dead in my father's chapel.   I sat beside him
all day and all night.   Just before daylight —
He breaks off abruptly.

RHODA.

Go on!

MICHAELIS.

Just before daylight, when the other watchers were asleep, the power of the spirit came strong upon me. I bowed myself upon the boy's body, and prayed.   My heart burned within me, for I felt his heart begin to beat!   His eyes opened. I told him to arise, and he arose.   He that was dead arose and was alive again!

Pause. Mrs. Beeler's bell rings. Michaelis starts, looks about him as if awakened from a dream, then slowly goes toward the hall door. Rhoda follows and detains him.

RHODA.

In a low tone.

How long had he lain — for dead?

MICHAELIS.

Three days.

RHODA.

With hesitation.

I have heard that people have lain as long as that in a trance, breathing so lightly that it could not be told, except by holding a glass before the face.

MICHAELIS.

Startled.

Is that true?

RHODA.

I have read so.

MICHAELIS.

I wonder — I wonder.

He stands in deep thought.

But I have had other signs.

RHODA.

What other signs?

MICHAELIS.

Many, many.   Up and down the land!

Pause.

I wonder. — I — I almost wish it were so!

*With bent head he goes out.   Rhoda stands looking after him
   until the inner door closes, then sits before the fire in revery.
   Beeler comes in from the barn.   He wears his old fur cap,
   and holds in one hand a bulky Sunday newspaper, in the
   other some battered harness, an awl, twine, and wax, which
   he deposits on the window seat.   He lays the paper on the
   table, and unfolds from it a large colored print, which he
   holds up and looks at with relish.*

Beeler.

These Sunday papers do get up fine supplements. I wouldn't take money for that picture.

Rhoda.

Looks at it absently.

What does it mean?

Beeler.

Reads.

" Pan and the Pilgrim." Guess you never heard of Pan, did you?

Rhoda.

Yes. One of the old heathen gods.

Beeler.

Call him heathen if you like! The folks that worshipped him thought he was orthodox, I guess.

He pins up the print, which represents a palmer of crusading times surprised in the midst of a forest by the god Pan.

Rhoda.

What does the picture mean?

BEELER.

Well, Pan there, he was a kind of a nature god.
The old Romans thought him out, to stand for
a lot of things.

RHODA.

What kind of things?

BEELER.

Natural things, with plenty of sap and mischie'
in 'em.   Growin' plants, and frisky animals, and
young folks in love.

He points to the figure of Pan, then to the Pilgrim, as he talks.

There he sits playin' Jenny-come-kiss-me on his
dod-gasted mouth-organ, when along comes one
of them fellows out of a monastery, with religion
on the brain.   Pikin' for Jerusalem, to get a
saint's toe-nail and a splinter of the true cross.

*Martha enters from the kitchen and potters about the room
   " redding up."*

Look at him!   Do you think he'll ever get to
Jerusalem?   Not this trip!   He hears the
pipes o' Pan.   He hears women callin' and
fiddles squeakin' love-tunes in the woods.   It'll
take more than a monk's robe on his back and
a shaved head on his shoulders to keep him

straight, I reckon. He'll call to mind that
young fellows had blood in their veins when
Adam was a farmer, and whoop-la! he'll be off
to the county fair, to dance ring-around-a-rosy
with Matildy Jane!

Pause, as he takes off his cap and lights his pipe.

Like to see our friend Michaelis meet up with
Mr. Pan. Don't believe Michaelis ever looked
cross-eyed at a girl.

He examines Rhoda quizzically.

You wouldn't make up bad as Matildy Jane
yourself, Rho, but sufferin' Job, he can't tell the
difference between crow's feet and dimples!

MARTHA.

Don't you be so sure!

BEELER.

Hello! Dan'el come to judgment! Never
seen an old maid yet that couldn't squeeze a
love story out of a flat-iron.

MARTHA.

I may be an old maid, and you may be an old
wind-bag, but I've got eyes in my head.

To Rhoda.

Where did you meet up with him, anyway?

Rhoda, plunged in thought, does not answer.

BEELER.

Wake up, Rhody! Marthy asked you where you met up with our new boarder.

RHODA.

On the road, coming home from the village.

BEELER.

What made you bring him here?

RHODA.

He wanted a quiet place to stay, and this was the best I knew.

MARTHA.

Guess it was! — A snap for him.

She goes out by the hall door.

RHODA.

Rises, takes the lamp off the mantel, and during the following cleans and refills it.

BEELER.

As he takes off his coat, and hangs it up.

Rhody, ain't this religious business rather a new thing with you? Up there in St. Louis, didn't go in for it much up there, did you?

RHODA.

Looks at him quickly.

Why do you ask that?

BEELER.

Oh, I gathered, from things I heard, that you cared more about dancin' than about prayin', up there.

She turns away.

That young fellow that was so sweet on you in St. Louis year before last, he wa'n't much in the psalm-singin' line, was he?

RHODA.

Startled and pale.

Who told you about him?

BEELER.

Oh, Mary's friends, the Higginses, used to write us about your affairs.   We thought it would be a hitch-up, sure as shootin'.   Studyin' to be a doctor, wasn't he?

RHODA.

Uncle, please never speak to me about him again!

BEELER.

All right, all right, my girl. I've been young myself, and I know youth is touchy as a gum-boil when it comes to love affairs. So it's all off, is it?

RHODA.

Yes.

BEELER.

Sits down to mend the harness.

If you're partial to the pill trade, we've got a brand new doctor in town now. Took old Doctor Martin's place. He'll be up here to see Mary in a day or two, and you can look him over.

RHODA.

What is his name?

BEELER.

Tries in vain to recall it.

Blamed if I can remember. Only seen him once. But I tell you, he's smart as tacks. Chuck full of Jamaica ginger. The very kind I'd have swore you'd take to, a while back, before you lost your fun and your spirit. When I first saw you on your father's farm out in Kansas, you was as wild a little gypsy as I ever set eyes on.   I said then to your dad, " There's a filly that'll need a good breakin'."   I never thought I'd see you takin' up with these Gospel pedlers.

*Martha comes in from the hall and fusses about, dusting, etc.
She points in the direction of Mrs. Beeler's room.*

MARTHA.

They're prayer-meetin' it again.   And Mary lyin' there as if she saw the pearly gates openin' before her eyes.

BEELER.

Half to himself as he works.

Poor Mary! — Mary's a strange woman.

MARTHA.

To Rhoda.

Your mother was the same way, Rhody.   The whole Beardsley tribe, for that matter.   But Mary was the worst.   It begun with Mary as soon as her brother Seth got drowned.

BEELER.

Looks up, angry.

None of that, Sis!

MARTHA.

I guess my tongue's my own.

BEELER.

No, it ain't. I won't have any more of that
'alk around me, do you hear? I put my foot
down a year ago.

MARTHA.

Points to his foot derisively.

It's big enough and ugly enough, Heaven knows,
but you can put it down as hard as you like, it
won't keep a man's sperrit in his grave — not
when he's a mind to come out!

BEELER.

Astonished.

Martha Beeler!

MARTHA.

That's my name.

*She flounces out into the kitchen, covering her retreat with
her last speech.*

BEELER.

Looking after her.

My kingdom! Martha! I thought she had
some horse sense left.

RHODA.

Slowly, as she finishes with the lamp.

Uncle, it's hard to live side by side with Aunt Mary and not —

BEELER.

In angry challenge.

And not what?

RHODA.

And not believe there's something more in these matters than "horse sense" will account for.

BEELER.

Hotly, as if a sore point has been touched upon.

There's nothing more than science will account for.

He points to a shelf of books.

You can read it up any day you like.   Read that book yonder, chapter called Hallucinations. Pathological, that's what it is, pathological.

RHODA.

What does that mean?

Beeler taps his forehead significantly.

Uncle, you know that's not true!

BEELER.

Growls to himself.

Pathological, up and down.

Rhoda replaces the lamp on the mantel.
Martha opens the kitchen door and calls in.

MARTHA.

Here's Uncle Abe!

BEELER.

Uncle Abe?   Thought he was a goner.

Uncle Abe enters.   He is an old negro, with gray hair and thin, gray beard.   He is somewhat bowed, and carries a stick, but he is not decrepit.   His clothes are spattered with mud.   Martha enters with him; she is stirring something in a bowl, and during the following continues to do so, though more and more interruptedly and absent-mindedly.

BEELER.

Hello, Uncle Abe.

UNCLE ABE.

Good-mawnin', Mista Beeler.

BEELER.

Where've you been all winter?   Thought you'd gone up Salt River.

Uncle Abe.

Shakes his head reassuringly.

Ain' nevah goin' up no Salt River, yo' Uncle Abe ain't.

Beeler.

Indicating Rhoda.

Make you acquainted with my wife's niece, Miss Williams.

Uncle Abe bows.

Rhoda.

Pushing forward a chair.

Sit down, Uncle. I don't see how you found your way in this dreadful fog.

Uncle Abe.

Fawg don' matta' nothin' to me, honey. Don' mean nothin' 'tall.

He speaks with exaltation and restrained excitement.

Yo' ol' Uncle keeps on tellin' 'em, dis hyah fawg an' darkness don' mean nothin' 'tall!

Rhoda and Martha look at him puzzled.
Beeler, busy over his harness, has not been struck by the old negro's words.

Beeler.

How's the ginseng crop this year?

UNCLE ABE.

They ain' no mo' gimsing!

BEELER.

No more ginseng?   What do you mean?

UNCLE ABE.

De good Lawd, he ain' goin' fool roun' no mo' wif no gimsing!

BEELER.

Amused.

Why, I thought your ginseng bitters was His main holt.

UNCLE ABE.

With a touch of regret.

Use to be, Mars' Beeler.   It shore use to be. —Yes, sah.   Bless de Lawd!

Shakes his head in reminiscence.

He sartinly did set sto' by them thah bitters.

BEELER.

With lazy amusement.

So the Lord's gone back on ginseng now, has He?

UNCLE ABE.

Yes, sah.

BEELER.

What makes you think so?

UNCLE ABE.

Solemnly.

Roots all kill by de fros'!

His manner grows more and more mysterious; he half closes his eyes, as he goes on in a strange, mounting singsong.

Knowed it more'n a monf ago, fo' dis hyah blin' worl' lef' de plough in de ploughshare an' de un- groun' wheat betwixen de millstones, and went a-follerin' aftah dis hyah new star outen de Eas', like a bride follerin' aftah de bridegroom!

Martha taps her forehead significantly, and goes back to her batter.

BEELER.

New star, Uncle?   Tell us about it.   Sounds interesting.

UNCLE ABE.

Stares at each of them in turn.

Ain' you-all heerd?

BEELER.

You've got the advantage of us.

UNCLE ABE.

Ain' you-all heerd 'bout de Healer?

BEELER.

Healer?   What kind of a healer?

UNCLE ABE.

With mounting indignation at Beeler's tone.

De Bible kin', dat's what kin'!   De kin' what
makes de lame fer to walk, and de blin' fer to
see, an' de daid fer to riz up outen their daid
col' graves.   That's what kin'!   Mean to say
you-all ain' heerd nothin' 'bout him, you po'
chillun o' dawkness?

*Martha and Beeler look at each other in amazement.   Rhoda
sits looking at the old negro, white and tense with excitement.*

BEELER.

Nope.

Recollecting.

Hold on!

MARTHA.

To Beeler.

Don't you remember, in the papers, two or
three weeks ago?   Where was it?   Some-
wheres out West.

BEELER.

Believe I did read some such goin's-on.   Don't
pay much attention to such nonsense.

Uncle Abe.

Solemn and threatening.

Tek keer, Mistah Beeler! Tek keer what you say 'fore dese here cloudy witnesses. Don' you go cuttin' yo'self off from de Kingdom. Nor you, Mis' Martha, nor you, honey. Don' ye do it! It's a-comin'. Yo' ol' Uncle Abe he's seen and heerd.

Rhoda.

Tell us quickly what you mean!

Uncle Abe.

Mean jes' what I says, honey. Night fo' last, de Healer, he come, like's if he jes' plum' drop from de sky.

More mysteriously.

An' whar's he gone to? You listen to yo' ol' Uncle Abe a-tellin' you. He ain' gone no-whars! He's jes' meechin' roun' in de fawg, a-waitin' fer de Lawd to call folks. En He's a-callin' 'em! He's a-callin' 'em by tens an' by hundreds. Town's full a'ready, honey. Main Street look jes' lak a fiel' hospital, down Souf durin' de wah!

MARTHA.

Meeting Beeler's astonished look.

What did I tell you? Maybe you'll listen to *me* next time.

RHODA.

To Uncle Abe, in a low, agitated voice.

This man you call the Healer — is he alone?

UNCLE ABE.

No, honey; folks says he don' nevah go nowheres by hisse'f. Always got that thah young man wif 'im what he raise from de daid.

BEELER.

Rises, with a shrug.

Good evening!

He crosses to the portraits of Darwin and Spencer.

You made quite a stir in your time, didn't you? Well, it's all up with you!

MARTHA.

In a voice strident with nervousness.

Raised from the dead?

UNCLE ABE.

That's what they says, Mis' Martha. Folks calls 'im Laz'rus in ref'ence to de Bible chil'

what riz up jes' same way lak', outen de daid
col' tomb.

*The Indian boy enters from the kitchen, his shoes and trousers
spattered with mud. Uncle Abe looks at him, then at the
others, and whispers to Rhoda. Martha bustles forward,
hiding her agitation in scolding speech.*

MARTHA.

Well, did you get my coffee and my sal-soda?

Lazarus points, without speaking, to the kitchen.

BEELER.

To Martha.

Did you send him to the store?

MARTHA.

Yes, I did send him to the store. If I had my
way, I'd send him — further.

*The boy hesitates, then goes stolidly out by the stair door.
Uncle Abe lifts his arm ecstatically.*

UNCLE ABE.

That's him! I tell ye that's the chil' what's said
"Howdy" to the daid folks down yonder. I'se
seen 'im in my dreams, an' now I'se seen 'im
wif dese hyah two eyes. — O Lawd, bless dis
hyah house o' grace!

BEELER.

I guess it's about time that fellow come out and exploded some of this tomfoolery.

He starts towards his wife's room.

RHODA.

Stopping him.

Please don't.

BEELER.

Peevishly.

There's got to be an end to this hoodoo business in my house.

Annie enters from the kitchen, dabbled with dye. She holds two colored eggs in her hands.

ANNIE.

Look!   I've colored two.

MARTHA.

Good gracious, child.   What a mess!

ANNIE.

Pa!   Play crack with me!   Just once, to see how it goes.

BEELER.

Go in and ask your mother if she'll let you.

Annie, her eggs in her apron, opens the hall door.   About to pass out, she stops, drops the eggs with a scream, and runs back, gazing towards the hall as she takes refuge behind Rhoda's skirts.

ANNIE.

Pa! Auntie! Ma's walking!

Mrs. Beeler enters, walking uncertainly, her face full of intense exaltation.   Michaelis comes just behind her, transfigured by spiritual excitement.

BEELER AND MARTHA.

Starting forward.

Mary!

RHODA.

Aunt Mary!

Mrs. Beeler advances into the room, reaching out her hand to Annie, who takes it in speechless fright.   She bends over and kisses the child's head, then stretches out her other hand to her husband.

MRS. BEELER.

Mat, I'm cured! The Lord has heard our prayers, for His saint's sake.

BEELER.

Why, Mary, I can't believe this—it's too—it's not possible!

Mrs. Beeler.

Looking at Michaelis.

It is written that he who has faith, even as a grain of mustard seed —.   I have had faith.

Martha.

Law, you've had faith enough any time these five years, Mary.   There was something else wanting, 'pears to me.

Mrs. Beeler.

There was wanting the word of true belief, saying, "Suffer no more!   Stoop and drink of the waters of mercy and healing."

Outside, the shrill soprano of a woman is heard, taking up a hymn.   At the sound Michaelis goes to the window.   He stands rigid, listening to the hymn to the end of the verse, when other voices join in the chorus.   The fog has partially cleared.

Michaelis.

Turning slowly to Rhoda.

Who are they?

Rhoda.

Sick people.

Michaelis.

How did they find out I was here?

RHODA.

It was known you were somewhere near. — They have been gathering for days. — They saw the boy, just now, in the village.

MRS. BEELER.

Comes a step or two nearer Michaelis.

Your great hour is at hand!

He looks distractedly about. The light has faded from his face, giving place to strong nervous agitation, resembling fear. He speaks as if to himself.

MICHAELIS.

My hour! — My hour! — And I — and I —!

He puts his hand over his eyes, as if to shut out some vision of dread.

MRS. BEELER.

You will not fail them? You cannot fail them, now.

Michaelis looks at Mrs. Beeler, then for a long time at Rhoda. He gathers himself together, and gazes steadfastly before him, as at some unseen presence.

No. — I have waited so long. I have had such deep assurances. — I must not fail. I must not fail.

CURTAIN

ACT II

ACT II

Late afternoon of the same day.

Mrs. Beeler sits in a low chair near the window. She has ceased reading the Testament, which lies open in her lap.

Uncle Abe sits on the floor with Annie. They are playing with building blocks, piling up and tearing down various ambitious structures. Rhoda enters from outside, with hat and cloak, carrying a large bunch of Easter lilies.

RHODA.

Kissing her aunt.

Still sitting up! You're not strong enough yet to do this. See, I've brought you some Easter lilies.

She hands one to Mrs. Beeler. As she takes off her things, she sees the old Negro gazing at her.

Well, Uncle Abe?

UNCLE ABE.

I's awake an' a-watchin', honey!

He turns again to the child, shaking his head as at some unspoken thought, while Rhoda arranges the flowers in a vase.

MRS. BEELER.

Rhoda!

RHODA.

Yes, Aunt Mary?

MRS. BEELER.

Come here.

Rhoda approaches. Mrs. Beeler speaks low, with suppressed excitement.

What is the news, outside?

RHODA.

You mustn't excite yourself. You must keep your strength.

MRS. BEELER.

I shall be strong enough.—Are the people still gathering from the town?

RHODA.

Yes, and they keep coming in from other places.

MRS. BEELER.

Are there many of them?

RHODA.

Many! Many! It's as if the whole world knew.

MRS. BEELER.

The more there are, the greater will be the witness.—*Pause.* When do you think he will go out to them?

RHODA.

They believe he is waiting for Easter morning.

Martha enters from kitchen, with bonnet and shawl on, and a large basket in her hand.

MARTHA.

Mary, you'd ought to be abed. You're tempting Providence.

She takes off her bonnet and shawl, and deposits the basket.

I saw your doctor down in the village, and he allowed he'd come up to see you this afternoon. He was all on end about your bein' able to walk.

RHODA.

I didn't know till to-day you had a doctor.

MRS. BEELER.

Yes.   He's a young man who's just come here to build up a practice.

MARTHA.

To Rhoda.

You better finish packin' the basket.   There's a lot o' hungry mouths to feed out yonder.

Exit by hall door.   Rhoda continues the preparation of the basket, taking articles from the cupboard and packing

*them.   Annie has climbed on a chair by the picture of Pan
and the Pilgrim.   She points at the figure of Pan.*

ANNIE.

Uncle Abe, tell me who that is.

UNCLE ABE.

Glancing at Mrs. Beeler and Rhoda.

H'sh!

ANNIE.

What's he doing up there in the bushes, blowing on that funny whistle?

UNCLE ABE.

Look hyah, chil', you jus' wastin' my time.   I
got frough wif dis hyah fool pictuh long 'go!

He tries to draw her away; she resists.

ANNIE.

Petulantly.

Uncle Abe!   Who is it?

UNCLE ABE.

Whispers, makes big eyes.

That thah's Ole Nick, that's who that thah is!
That thah's de Black Man!

*Annie, terror-stricken, jumps down and retreats to her moth-
er's chair. Mrs. Beeler rouses from her revery and
strokes her child's head.*

MRS. BEELER.

Oh, my child, how happy you are to see this
while you are so young! You will never forget,
will you, dear?

ANNIE.

Fidgeting.

Forget what?

MRS. BEELER.

Tell me that whatever happens to you in the
world, you won't forget that once, when you
were a little girl, you saw the heavens standing
open, and felt that God was very near, and full
of pity for His children.

ANNIE.

I don't know what you're talking about!   I can't
hardly breathe the way people are in this house.

MRS. BEELER.

You will understand, some day, what wonderful
things your childish eyes looked on.

*Annie retreats to Uncle Abe, who bends over the child and
whispers in her ear. She grows amused, and begins to
sway as to a tune, then chants.*

ANNIE.

" Mary an' a' Martha's jus' gone along,
    Mary an' a' Martha's jus' gone along,
    Mary an' a' Martha's jus' gone along,
        Ring dem charmin' bells."

*As she finishes the rhyme she runs out into the hall. Mrs.
    Beeler begins again to read her Testament. The old negro
    approaches Mrs. Beeler and Rhoda, and speaks myste-
    riously.*

UNCLE ABE.

That thah chil' she's talkin' sense. They's
sumpin' ain't right about dis hyah house.

MRS. BEELER.

Not right?   What do you mean?

UNCLE ABE.

Shakes his head dubiously.

Dunno, Mis' Beeler.   I's jes' a ole fool colored
pusson, been waitin' fer de great day what de
'Postle done promise.   En hyah's de great day
'bout to dawn, an' de Lawd's Chosen 'bout to
show Hisse'f in clouds o' glory 'fore de worl', an'
lo 'n' behol' —

He leans closer and whispers.

de Lawd's Chosen One, he's done got a spell
on 'im!

Mrs. Beeler.

Shocked and startled.

Uncle Abe!

Uncle Abe.

Pointing at the Pan and the Pilgrim.

Why do you keep that thah pictuh nail up thah fur?

Mrs. Beeler.

My husband likes it.

Uncle Abe.

Mighty funny kin' o' man, like to hev de Black Man lookin' pop-eyed at folks all day an' all night, puttin' de spell on folks!

Mrs. Beeler.

That's not the Black Man.

Uncle Abe.

That's him, shore's yo' born! Jes' what he looks like. I's seen 'im, more'n once.

Rhoda.

Seen the Black Man, Uncle?

Uncle Abe.

Yais, ma'am. I's spied 'im, sittin' in de paw-paw bushes in de springtime, when de snakes a-runnin', an' de jays a-hollerin', and de crick a-talkin' sassy to hisse'f.

He leans nearer, more mysteriously.

En what you s'pose I heerd him whis'lin', for all de worl' lak dem scan'lous bluejays?

Chants in a high, trilling voice.

"Chillun, chillun, they ain' no Gawd, they ain' no sin nor no jedgment, they's jes' springtime an' happy days, and folks carryin' on. Whar's yo' lil gal, Abe Johnson?   Whar's yo' lil sweet-heart gal?"   An' me on'y got religion wintah befo', peekin' roun' pie-eyed, skeered good.   En fo' you could say "De Lawd's my Shepherd," kerchunk goes de Black Man in de mud-puddle, change' into a big green bullfrog!

Mrs. Beeler.

You just imagined all that.

Uncle Abe.

Indignant.

Jes' 'magine!   Don' I know de Devil when I sees him, near 'nough to say "Howdy"?

MRS. BEELER.

There isn't any Devil.

UNCLE ABE.

Astounded.

Ain't no Devil?

MRS. BEELER.

No.

Uncle Abe goes, with puzzled headshakings, towards the kitchen door. He stops to smell the Easter lilies, then raises his head and looks at her again, with puzzled scrutiny.

UNCLE ABE.

Mis' Beelah, did I understan' you to say — they ain' — no Devil?

MRS. BEELER.

Touching her breast.

Only here, Uncle Abe.

The old negro stares at her and Rhoda, and goes into the kitchen, feeling his own breast and shaking his head dubiously. Mrs. Beeler looks at the picture.

Do you think your Uncle Mat would mind if we took that picture down?

Rhoda unpins the picture from the wall, rolls it up, and lays it on the bookshelf. Her aunt goes on, hesitatingly.

Do you know, Rhoda, I have sometimes thought — You won't be hurt?

RHODA.

No.

MRS. BEELER.

I—I know what that old negro says is all fool-
ishness, but—there *is* something the matter
with Mr. Michaelis.   Have you noticed?

RHODA.

Avoiding her aunt's gaze.

Yes.

MRS. BEELER.

Just when his great work is about to begin!—
What do you think it can be?

RHODA.

How should I know, Aunt Mary?

MRS. BEELER.

I thought maybe — Rhoda, I have seen him
look at you so strangely!   Like—like the
Pilgrim in the picture, when he hears that
heathen creature playing on the pipe. —
You are such a wild creature, or you used
to be.

Rhoda comes to her aunt and stands a moment in silence.

RHODA.

Auntie.

MRS. BEELER.

Yes?

RHODA.

I think I ought to go away.

MRS. BEELER.

Astonished.

Go away?   Why?

RHODA.

So as not to—hinder him.

MRS. BEELER.

Caressing her.

There, you have taken what I said too seriously.
It was only a sick woman's imagination.

RHODA.

No, it was the truth.   You see it, though you
try not to.   Even Uncle Abe sees it.   Just
when Mr. Michaelis most needs his strength,
weakness has come upon him.

MRS. BEELER.

You mean—?

She hesitates.

You mean — because of you? — Rhoda, look at me.

Rhoda avoids her aunt's gaze; Mrs. Beeler draws down the girl's face and gazes at it.

Is there anything — that I don't know — between you and him?

RHODA.

I — I must go away. — I ought to have gone before.

MRS. BEELER.

My child, this — this troubles me very much. He is different from other men, and you — and you —

RHODA.

With passion.

Say it, say it! What am I?

MRS. BEELER.

Don't be hurt, Rhoda, but — you have a wild nature. You are like your father. I remember when he used to drive over to see sister Jane, with his keen face and eagle eyes, behind his span of wild colts, I used to tremble for my gentle sister. You are just like him, or you used to be.

Rhoda breaks away from her aunt, and takes her hat and cloak.   Mrs. Beeler rises with perturbation, and crosses to detain her.

What are you going to do?

RHODA.

I am going away — I *must* go away.
Martha enters from the hall.

MRS. BEELER.
Speaks lower.
Promise me you won't!   Promise me!

MARTHA.

To look at that, now!   Seein' you on your feet, Mary, gives me a new start every time.

MRS. BEELER.
To Rhoda.
You promise?
Rhoda bows her head as in assent.

MARTHA.

Doctor's in the parlor.   Shall I bring him in here?

MRS. BEELER.

No.   I think I will rest awhile.   He can come to my room.

She walks unsteadily.   The others try to help her, but she motions them back.

No.   It's so good to feel that I can walk alone!

MARTHA.

It does beat all!

MRS. BEELER.

I'll just lie down on the couch.   I want to go out, before dark, and speak to the people.

Mr. Beeler enters from the kitchen and crosses to help his wife.   The others give place to him.

Oh Mat, our good days are coming back!   I shall be strong and well for you again.

BEELER.

Yes, Mary.   There will be nothing to separate us any more.

MRS. BEELER.

Points at his books.

Not even — them?

He goes to the alcove, takes the books from the shelf, raises the lid of the window-seat, and throws them in.

Mrs. Beeler points to the pictures of Darwin and Spencer.

Nor them?

He unpins the pictures, lays them upon the heap of books, and returns to her.

You don't know how happy that makes me!

They go out by the hall door.   Martha, as she lowers the lid of the window-seat, points derisively at the heap.

MARTHA.

That's a good riddance of bad rubbish!

She comes to the table and continues packing the basket.

You'd better help me with this basket.   Them folks will starve to death, if the neighborhood round don't give 'em a bite to eat.

Rhoda fetches other articles from the cupboard.

I'd like to know what they think we are made of, with butter at twenty-five cents a pound and flour worth its weight in diamonds!

RHODA.

All the neighbors are helping, and none of them with our cause for thankfulness.

MARTHA.

That's no sign you should go plasterin' on that butter like you was a bricklayer tryin' to bust the contractor!

She takes the bread from Rhoda and scrapes the butter thin.

RHODA.

As the clock strikes five.

It's time for Aunt Mary to have her tea.　Shall I make it?

MARTHA.

You make it!　Not unless you want to lay her flat on her back again!

As she flounces out, Annie enters from the hall.　She points with one hand at the retreating Martha, with the other toward her mother's room.

ANNIE.

Sings with sly emphasis.

" Mary an' a' Martha's jus' gone along,
　　Mary an' a' Martha's jus' gone along,
　　Mary an' a' Martha's jus' gone along,
　　　Ring dem charmin' bells."

She climbs upon a chair by the table, and fingers the contents of basket as she sings.

RHODA.

What's got into you, little imp?

ANNIE.

Brazenly.

I've been peeping through mamma's keyhole.

RHODA.

That's not nice.

ANNIE.

I know it, but the minister's in there and Dr. Littlefield.

RHODA.

Startled.

Who?

ANNIE.

You know, mamma's doctor.— Oh, he's never come since you've been here.

RHODA.

In a changed voice, as she takes the child by the shoulders.

What does he look like?

ANNIE.

Don't, you're hurting me!— He's too red in the face, and looks kind of — insulting — and he wears the most *beautiful* neckties, and —

Exhausted by her efforts at description.

Oh, I don't know!

She sings as she climbs down, and goes out by the kitchen door.

> " Free grace, undyin' love,
>   Free grace, undyin' love,
>   Free grace, undyin' love,
>   Ring dem lovely bells."

Dr. Littlefield enters from Mrs. Beeler's room. He speaks back to Beeler on the threshold.

LITTLEFIELD.

Don't bother! I'll find it.

Looking for something, he approaches Rhoda, who has her back turned.

Beg pardon. Have you seen a pocket thermometer I left here?

She faces him. He starts back in surprise.

Bless my soul and body! Rhoda Williams!

He closes the hall door, returns to her, and stands somewhat disconcerted.

Here, of all places!

RHODA.

Mrs. Beeler is my aunt.

LITTLEFIELD.

Well, well! The world is small. — Been here long?

RHODA.

Only a month.

LITTLEFIELD.

And before that?

RHODA.

It's a long story.   Besides, you wouldn't understand.

LITTLEFIELD.

You might let me try.   What in the world
have you been doing all this time?

RHODA.

I have been searching for something.

LITTLEFIELD.

What was it?

RHODA.

My own lost self.   My own — lost soul.

LITTLEFIELD.

Amused at her solemnity.

You're a queer bundle of goods.   Always
were.   Head full of solemn notions about life,
and at the same time, when it came to a lark, —
Oh, I'm no grandmother, but when you got on
your high horse — well!

He waves his hands expressively.

RHODA.

Bursts out.

The great town, the people, the noise, and the lights — after seventeen years of life on a dead prairie, where I'd hardly heard a laugh or seen a happy face! — All the same, the prairie had me still.

LITTLEFIELD.

You don't mean you went back to the farm?

RHODA.

I mean that the years I'd spent out there in that endless stretch of earth and sky —.

She breaks off, with a weary gesture.

There's no use going into that.   You wouldn't understand.

LITTLEFIELD.

No, I walk on simple shoe leather and eat mere victuals. — Just the same, it wasn't square of you to clear out that way — vanish into air without a word or a sign.

RHODA.

Looking at him steadily.

You know very well why I went.

LITTLEFIELD.

Returning her gaze, unabashed, chants with meaning and relish.

" Hey diddle, diddle,
   The cat and the fiddle,
   The cow jumped over the moon."

Rhoda takes up the basket and goes toward the outer door. He intercepts her.

RHODA.

Let me pass.

LITTLEFIELD.

You're not taking part in this camp-meeting enthusiasm, are you?

RHODA.

Yes.

As he stares at her, his astonishment changes to amusement; he chuckles to himself, then bursts out laughing, as in humorous reminiscence.

LITTLEFIELD.

Bless my soul! And to think that only a couple of little years ago — Oh, *bless* my soul!

The stair door opens. Michaelis appears. His face is flushed, his hair disordered, and his whole person expresses a feverish and precarious exaltation.

MICHAELIS.

Looks at Littlefield with vague query, then at Rhoda.

Excuse me, I am very thirsty. I came down for a glass of water.

Rhoda goes to the kitchen door, where she turns. The doctor puts on a pair of nose-glasses and scans Michaelis with interest. He holds out his hand, which Michaelis takes.

LITTLEFIELD.

We ought to know each other. We're colleagues, in a way.

MICHAELIS.

Colleagues?

LITTLEFIELD.

In a way, yes. I'm a practising physician.

Exit Rhoda.

You seem to have the call on us professionals, to judge by the number of your clients out yonder.

He points out of the window.

To say nothing of Exhibit One!

He points to the hall door.

MICHAELIS.

Vaguely.

I — I don't know that I —

Rhoda enters from the kitchen, with water, which he takes.

Thank you.

*He drinks thirstily.   Mr. Beeler appears in the hall door;
he looks at the group, taken aback.*

BEELER.

Oh — !

LITTLEFIELD.

I stopped to chat with your niece.   She and I
happen to be old acquaintances.

BEELER.

You don't say? — Would you mind coming in
here for a minute?

LITTLEFIELD.

Following him out.

What's up?

BEELER.

My wife's got it in her head that she's called
upon to —

*Door closes.   Michaelis, who has followed Littlefield with
his eyes, sets down the glass, and turns slowly to Rhoda.*

MICHAELIS.

Who is that?

RHODA.

My aunt's doctor.

MICHAELIS.

You know him well?

RHODA.

Yes. — No.

MICHAELIS.

What does that mean?

RHODA.

I haven't seen him for nearly two years. — I
can't remember much about the person I was,
two years ago.

MICHAELIS.

Yes! Yes! I understand.

He turns away, lifting his hands, speaking half to himself.

That these lives of ours should be poured like
a jelly, from one mould into another, until God
Himself cannot remember what they were two
years ago, or two hours ago!

RHODA.

Why do you say that?

*He does not answer, but walks nervously about. Rhoda,
watching him, speaks, after a silence.*

Last month — out West — were there many
people there?

MICHAELIS.

No. — Two or three.

RHODA.

The papers said —

MICHAELIS.

When the crowd began to gather, I — went
away.

RHODA.

Why?

MICHAELIS.

My time had not come.
He has stopped before the map and stands gazing at it.

RHODA.

Has it come now?
She comes closer.
— Has your time come now?

MICHAELIS.

Yes.

RHODA.

How do you know?

MICHAELIS.

Points at the map.
It is written there!

RHODA.

How do you mean, written there?

MICHAELIS.

Can't you see it?

RHODA.

I see the map, nothing more.

MICHAELIS.

Points again, gazing fixedly.

It seems to me to be written in fire.

RHODA.

What seems written?

MICHAELIS.

What I have been doing, all these five years.

RHODA.

Since your work began?

MICHAELIS.

It has never begun. Many times I have thought,
" Now," and some man or woman has risen up
healed, and looked at me with eyes of prophecy.

But a Voice would cry, "On, on!" and I would go forward, driven by a force and a will not my own. — I didn't know what it all meant, but I know now.

He points at the map, his manner transformed with excitement and exaltation.

It is written there.   It is written in letters of fire.   My eyes are opened, and I see!

RHODA.

Following his gaze, then looking at him again, awed and bewildered.

What is it that you see?

MICHAELIS.

The cross!

RHODA.

I — I don't understand.

MICHAELIS.

All those places where the hand was lifted for a moment, and the power flowed into me —

He places his finger at various points on the map; these points lie in two transverse lines, between the Mississippi and the Pacific; one line runs roughly north and south, the other east and west.

Look! There was such a place, and there another, and there, and there. And there was one, and there, and there. — Do you see?

RHODA.

I see. — It makes a kind of cross.

MICHAELIS.

You see it too! And do you see what it means — this sign that my feet have marked across the length and breadth of a continent?

He begins again to pace the room.

— And that crowd of stricken souls out yonder, raised up as by miracle, their broken bodies crying to be healed, — do you see what they mean?

RHODA.

In a steady voice.

They mean what my aunt said this morning. They mean that your great hour has come.

MICHAELIS.

My hour! my hour!

He comes nearer, and speaks in a quieter tone.

I knew a young Indian once, a Hopi boy, who made songs and sang them to his people. One evening we sat on the roof of the chief's house and asked him to sing. He shook his head, and went away in the starlight. The next morning, I found him among the rocks under the mesa, with an empty bottle by his side. — He never sang again! Drunkenness had taken him. He never sang again, or made another verse.

RHODA.

What has that to do with you? It's not —? You don't mean that you —?

MICHAELIS.

No. There is a stronger drink for such as I am!

RHODA.

Forcing herself to go on.

What — " stronger drink "?

MICHAELIS.

Wildly.

The wine of this world! The wine-bowl that crowns the feasting table of the children of this world.

RHODA.

What do you mean by — the wine of this world?

MICHAELIS.

You know that!   Every woman knows.

He points out of the window, at the sky flushed with sunset color.

Out there, at this moment, in city and country, souls, thousands upon thousands of souls, are dashing in pieces the cup that holds the wine of heaven, the wine of God's shed blood, and lifting the cups of passion and of love, that crown the feasting table of the children of this earth!   Look!   The very sky is blood-red with the lifted cups.   And we two are in the midst of them.   Listen what I sing there, on the hills of light in the sunset: " Oh, how beautiful upon the mountains are the feet of my beloved!"

A song rises outside, loud and near at hand — Michaelis listens, his expression gradually changing from passionate excitement to brooding distress.

Vaguely, as the music grows fainter and dies away.

I — we were saying — .

He grasps her arm in nervous apprehension.

For God's sake, tell me. — Are there many people — waiting — out there?

RHODA.

Hundreds, if not thousands.

MICHAELIS.

Walks about.

Thousands. — Thousands of thousands! —

He stops beside her.

You won't leave me alone?

RHODA.

Hesitates, then speaks with decision.

No.

MICHAELIS.

Continuing his walk.

Thousands of thousands!

The hall door opens, Dr. Littlefield and a Clergyman, the Rev. John Culpepper, enter. The latter stares inquiringly from Michaelis to the Doctor, who nods affirmatively, and adjusts his glasses.

CULPEPPER.

Mutters to Littlefield.

Nonsense!   Sacrilegious nonsense!

LITTLEFIELD.

Same tone.

I've done my best.

Behind them comes Mrs. Beeler, supported by her Husband. At the same moment Martha enters from the kitchen, with tea; Uncle Abe and Annie follow.

BEELER.

On the threshold.

Mary, take another minute to consider.

Mrs. Beeler, as if without hearing this protest, gazes at Michaelis, and advances into the room with a gesture of the arms which causes her supporter to loosen his hold, though he follows slightly behind, to render aid if necessary.

MRS. BEELER.

To Michaelis.

Tell me that I may go out, and stand before them for a testimony!

LITTLEFIELD.

As a physician, I must formally protest.

CULPEPPER.

And I as a minister of the Gospel.

MRS. BEELER.

To Michaelis, with a nervous, despairing gesture.

Speak to them! Explain to them! I am too weak.

There is a sound of excited voices outside, near at hand, then a sudden trample of footsteps at the entrance door. As Beeler goes hurriedly to the door it bursts open and a young woman with a baby in her arms crowds past him, and stands looking wildly about the room.

BEELER.

As he forces the others back.

You can't come in here, my friends! Stand back!

The woman gazes from one to another of the men. The old negro points at Michaelis. She advances to him, holding out the child.

MOTHER.

Don't let my baby die! For Christ's sake, don't let him die!

He examines the child's face, touches the mother's head tenderly, and signs to Rhoda to take them into the inner room.

MICHAELIS.

Take her with you, I will come.

RHODA.

With gentle urgency, to the woman.

Come with me.

She leads the woman out through the hall door.

MICHAELIS.

To Mrs. Beeler, as he points outside.

Tell them to wait until to-morrow at sunrise.

*Mr. and Mrs. Beeler move toward the entrance door; some
of the others start after, some linger, curious to know what
will happen to the child. Michaelis turns upon them
with a commanding gesture.*

Go, all of you!

*The room is cleared except for Littlefield, who goes last,
stops in the doorway, closes the door, and approaches
Michaelis. He speaks in a friendly and reasonable tone.*

LITTLEFIELD.

You're on the wrong track, my friend.

MICHAELIS.

I asked you to go.

LITTLEFIELD.

I heard you. I want to say a word or two first.
For your own sake and for that woman's sake,
you'd better listen. You can't do anything for
her baby.

MICHAELIS.

Is that for you to say?

LITTLEFIELD.

Yes, sir! It is most decidedly for me to say.

MICHAELIS.

By what authority?

LITTLEFIELD.

By the authority of medical knowledge. — You
are a very remarkable man, with a very remarkable gift. In your own field, I take off my hat
to you. If you knew yourself as science knows
you, you might make the greatest doctor living.
Your handling of Mrs. Beeler's case was mas-
terly. But — come right down to it — *you* didn't
work the cure.

MICHAELIS.

I know that.

LITTLEFIELD.

Who do you think did?

MICHAELIS.

Raising his hands.

He whom I serve, and whom you blaspheme!

LITTLEFIELD.

No, sir! He whom *I* serve, and whom *you*
blaspheme — Nature. Or rather, Mrs. Beeler
did it herself.

MICHAELIS.

Herself?

LITTLEFIELD.

You gave her a jog, so to speak, here, or here,
Touches his brain and heart.

and she did the rest.   But you can't do the same
to everybody. Above all, you can't do it to a baby
in arms.   There's nothing either here or here,

Touches brain and heart.

to get hold of.   I'm a modest man, and as I say,
in your own field you're a wonder.   But in a
case like this one —

He points to the hall door.

I'm worth a million of you.

MICHAELIS.

*Moves as if to give place to him, with a challenging gesture
    toward the door.*

Try !

LITTLEFIELD.

Shrugs.

Not much !   The woman wouldn't listen to me.
And if she did, and I failed — oh, I'm no miracle
worker ! — they'd make short work of me, out
there.

He points out and adds significantly.

They're in no mood for failures, out there.

*Michaelis's gaze, as if in spite of himself, goes to the window.
    He rests his hand on the table, to stop its trembling. Little-
    field goes on, watching him with interest.*

Nervously speaking, you are a high power machine. The dynamo that runs you is what is called "faith," "religious inspiration," or what-not. It's a dynamo which nowadays easily gets out of order. Well, my friend, as a doctor, I warn you that your little dynamo is out of order. — In other words, you've lost your grip. You're in a funk.

Rhoda opens the hall door and looks anxiously at the two. Michaelis approaches her with averted eyes. As he is about to pass out, she speaks timidly.

RHODA.

Do you want me?

MICHAELIS.

In a toneless voice.

No.

She watches him until the inner door shuts. She and Little-field confront each other in silence for a moment across the width of the room.

RHODA.

Forcing herself to speak calmly.

Please go.

LITTLEFIELD.

Drops his professional tone for one of cynical badinage.

You make up well as one of the Wise Virgins, whose lamps are trimmed and burning for the

bridegroom to pass by.   I hope that personage
won't disappoint you, nor the several hundred
others, out yonder, whose lamps are trimmed
and burning.

*The outer door opens.   Mrs. Beeler enters, supported by her
husband, and accompanied by Martha and the Rev. Culpepper, with Uncle Abe following in the rear.   Rhoda
hastens to her aunt's side.*

Mrs. Beeler.

Ah, Rhoda, I wish you had been out there with
me.   Such beautiful human faces ! Such poor,
suffering, believing human faces, lit up by such
a wonderful new hope!

She turns to the minister.

Wasn't it a wonderful thing to see?

Culpepper.

It is wonderful to see human nature so credu-
lous.   And to me, very painful.

Mrs. Beeler.

To-morrow you will see how right these poor
souls are to lift their trust so high. —

To Rhoda.

Where is he now?

Rhoda points in the direction of her own room.

How happy that young mother's heart will be to-night!

UNCLE ABE.

Solemnly.

Amen!

CULPEPPER.

In a dry tone.

We will hope so.

They move to the hall door, where Beeler resigns his wife to Rhoda.   The two pass out.

Culpepper, Littlefield, and Beeler remain.   During the following conversation, Martha lights the lamp, after directing Uncle Abe, by a gesture, to take the provision basket into the kitchen.   He does so.

LITTLEFIELD.

Pointing through the window.

They're just laying siege to you, ain't they?   I guess they won't let your man give them the slip, this time — even though you do let him run loose.

BEELER.

With severity.

You have seen my wife walk alone to-day, the first time in five years.

LITTLEFIELD.

I beg your pardon.   I understand how you feel about it.

Martha goes out into the kitchen.

And even if it proves to be only temporary —

BEELER.

Temporary!

LITTLEFIELD.

Permanent, let us hope.   Anyway, it's a very remarkable case.   Astonishing.   I've only known one just like it — personally, I mean.

BEELER.

Astounded.

Just like it?

LITTLEFIELD.

Well, pretty much.   Happened in Chicago when I was an interne at St. Luke's.

BEELER.

Then it's not — there's nothing — peculiar about it?

LITTLEFIELD.

Yes, sir-ree!   Mighty peculiar!

Beeler.

I mean nothing, as you might say, outside nature?

Littlefield.

O, bless you, you can't get outside nature now-adays!

Moves his hands in a wide circle.

Tight as a drum, no air-holes.—Devilish queer, though — pardon me, Mr. Culpepper — really amazing, the power of the mind over the body.

Culpepper.

Would you be good enough to let us hear some of your professional experiences?

Littlefield.

Lights a cigarette, as he leans on the edge of the table.

Don't have to go to professional medicine for cases.   They're lying around loose.   Why, when I was at Ann Arbor — in a fraternity initiation — we bared a chap's shoulders, showed him a white-hot poker, blindfolded him, told him to stand steady, and — touched him with a piece of ice.   A piece of ice, I tell you!   What happened?   Damned if it — pardon me, Mr.

Culpepper — blessed if it didn't *burn* him — carries the scars to this day. Then there was that case in Denver. Ever hear about that? A young girl, nervous patient. Nails driven through the palms of her hands, — tenpenny nails, — under the hypnotic suggestion that she wasn't being hurt. Didn't leave a cicatrice as big as a bee sting! Fact!

BEELER.

You think my wife's case is like these?

LITTLEFIELD.

Precisely; with religious excitement to help out. *He points outside.*

They're getting ready for Kingdom-come over it, out yonder, dear Dr. Culpepper.

BEELER.

They're worked up enough, if that's all that's needed.

LITTLEFIELD.

Worked up! Elijah in a chariot of fire, distributing cure-alls as he mounts to glory. They've got their ascension robes on, especially the niggers.

CULPEPPER.

With severity.

I take it you are the late Dr. Martin's successor.

LITTLEFIELD.

I have the honor.

CULPEPPER.

Old Dr. Martin would never have taken a flippant tone in such a crisis.

LITTLEFIELD.

Flippant?   By no means!   A little light-headed.
My profession is attacked.   At its very roots,
sir. —

With relish.

As far as that goes, I'm afraid yours is, too.

CULPEPPER.

To Beeler, ignoring the gibe.

Am I to understand that you countenance these
proceedings?

BEELER.

Pointing to the invalid chair.

If your wife had spent five years helpless in
that chair, I guess you'd countenance any proceedings that set her on her feet.

CULPEPPER.

Towers threateningly.

If your wife is the woman she was, she would rather sit helpless forever beside the Rock of Ages, than dance and flaunt herself in the house of idols!

BEELER.

With depreciating humor.

O, I guess she ain't doin' much flauntin' of herself in any house of idols. — You've heard Doctor here say it's all natural enough. Maybe this kind of cure is the coming thing.

LITTLEFIELD.

The Brother would drive us doctors into the poorhouse, if he could keep up the pace. And you preachers, too, as far as that goes. If he could keep up the pace! Well —

Sucks at his cigarette deliberately.

lucky for us, he *can't* keep it up.

BEELER.

Why can't he keep it up?

LITTLEFIELD.

Can't stand the strain. — Oh, I haven't seen him operate, but I'm willing to bet his miracles take it out of him!

CULPEPPER.

Takes his hat and goes toward the outer door.

Miracles, indeed!

LITTLEFIELD.

Following.

Oh, wait for me, Doctor; we're both in the same boat!

BEELER.

Hope you gentlemen will come back again to-night, and soon too.   Don't know what'll happen if things go wrong in there.

Points towards the hall.

LITTLEFIELD.

All right — you can count on me —

BEELER.

To Culpepper.

And you?

CULPEPPER.

I seldom shirk my duty.

Beeler closes the door after them.

Martha enters from the kitchen, with a pan of dough, which she sets before the fire to raise.

BEELER.

You keepin' an eye out, Marthy?

MARTHA.

Guess your barn'd 'a' been afire, if I hadn't been keepin' an eye out.

BEELER.

I warned 'em about fire!

MARTHA.

Haymow ketched. If I hadn't been there to put it out, we'd 'a' been without a roof by now.

BEELER.

Guess I better go keep an eye out myself.

MARTHA.

Guess you had!

Beeler goes out by the kitchen. Martha takes up mechanically her eternal task of setting things to rights — gathering up Annie's toys and arranging the furniture in more precise order. Meanwhile, Rhoda enters from the hall with the mother of the sick child, a frail young woman of nervous type. She clings to Rhoda feverishly.

MOTHER.

Don't leave me!

RHODA.

You mustn't worry.   Your baby will get well.

Rhoda sinks in a low easy chair before the fire, and the woman kneels beside her, her face hidden on the chair arm.

You must keep up your courage and your trust. That will help more than anything.

MOTHER.

I'm afraid!

RHODA.

Think of those others out there, who are waiting too, without the glimpse of comfort you've had.

MOTHER.

Bursts out.

I ain't had no comfort! When I heard him pray for my child, I — I don't know — I kept sayin' to myself — "O God, it's me that's stretchin' out my hands to you, not him. Don't punish me for his cold words!"

Martha, who has been listening, shakes her head significantly

RHODA.

Cold words!

MOTHER.

Yes, I know it's wrong. I'll try to feel different. It's because I ain't had nothin' to do with religion for so long. — If my baby gets well, I'll make up for it. I'll make up for everything.

The woman rises. Rhoda kisses her.

RHODA.

I shall be here if you want me. And I shall — pray for you.

The mother goes out. Distant singing is heard. Martha comes to the mantelpiece with matches, which she arranges in the match tray. She looks at Rhoda, who sits with closed eyes.

MARTHA.

Guess you're about dead beat.

RHODA.

I think I never was so tired in my life.

MARTHA.

Worry does it, more'n work. Better try and doze off, Rhody.

The hall door opens, and Annie enters. She comes to Martha, and clings nervously to her skirts.

ANNIE.

Aunt Martha! I want to stay with you. You're the only person in this house that ain't different. What's the matter with Mamma?

MARTHA.

She's cured, I reckon.

ANNIE.

How did she get cured?

MARTHA.

You can search me!

ANNIE.

Did that man cure her?

MARTHA.

That's what she says, and I don't hear him denyin' it.

ANNIE.

Whining.

I don't want her to be cured!

MARTHA.

Annie Beeler! Don't want your mother to be cured?

ANNIE.

No, I don't.   I want her to be like she always
has been.   She don't seem like my Mamma at
all this way.   What's the matter with all those
people out there?   Why don't we have any
supper?

She bursts out crying and clings feverishly to Martha.

Oh, what's going to happen to us?

MARTHA.

There, Annie, don't cry.

*She looks at Rhoda, throws a cover over her knees, and draws
    Annie away, speaking low.*

Come out in the kitchen, and I'll give you your
supper.

*Exeunt.   The singing grows louder and nearer.   Michaelis
    enters from the hall.   His hair is dishevelled, his collar open,
    his manner feverish and distraught.   He looks closely at
    Rhoda, sees she is sleeping, then paces the floor nervously,
    gazing out of the window in the direction of the singing.
    At length he comes to Rhoda again, and bends over her,
    studying her face.   She starts up, confused and terror-
    stricken, from her doze.*

RHODA.

What — what is the matter?   Oh, you frightened me so!

Michaelis turns away without answering.

What has happened?   Why are you here?

MICHAELIS.

You had dropped asleep.   You are weary.

RHODA.

Collecting her thoughts with difficulty.

I was dreaming — such a strange dream.

MICHAELIS.

What did you dream?

RHODA.

I thought it was morning; the sun had risen, and — and you were out there, in the midst of the crowd.

MICHAELIS.

Excitedly.

Go on!   What happened?

RHODA.

I — I can't remember the rest.

MICHAELIS.

Grasps her arm, speaks low.

You must remember!   Did I — succeed?

RHODA.

Helplessly.

I — it's all a blur in my mind.

MICHAELIS.

Darkly.

You don't want me to know that, in your dream, I failed.

RHODA.

No, no.   That is not so.

Pause.   She speaks with hesitation.

Perhaps this is not the time.   Perhaps you are not ready.

MICHAELIS.

What does that matter?   *He* is ready.

He points at the map.

RHODA.

Gazing at the map, with mystic conviction.

You will succeed!   You must succeed!

He paces the room.   She stops him, pointing toward the hall door.

How is the child?

He hesitates.   She repeats the words anxiously.

How is the child?

He shakes his head gloomily for answer.

It will get well, I am sure.

MICHAELIS.

If it does not, I am judged.

RHODA.

Oh, don't say that or think it!

MICHAELIS.

I am weighed in the balance and found wanting!

RHODA.

You cannot hang the whole issue and meaning
of your life upon so slight a thread.

MICHAELIS.

The whole issue and meaning of the world hang
on threads as slight.   If this one is slight.   To
the mother it is not slight, nor to the God who
put into her eyes, as she looked at me, all the
doubt and question of the suffering earth.

RHODA.

You must remember that it is only a little child.
Its mind is not open.   You cannot influence it
—can you?

MICHAELIS.

Once that little life in my hand would have been
as clay in the hands of the potter.   If I cannot

help now, it is because my ministry has been taken from me and given to another, who will be strong where I am weak, and faithful where I am unfaithful.

Another song rises outside, distant.

RHODA.

Comes closer to him.

Tell me this. Speak plainly to me. Is it because of me that your weakness and unfaith have come upon you? Is it because of me?

MICHAELIS.

Looking at her steadily.

Yes.—

He comes nearer.

Before creation, beyond time, God not yet risen from His sleep, you stand and call to me, and I listen in a dream that I dreamed before Eden.

RHODA.

Shrinking from him.

You must not say such things to me.—You must not think of me so.—You must not!

He follows her, his passion mounting.

MICHAELIS.

All my life long I have known you, and fled
from you.   I have heard you singing on the
hills of sleep and have fled from you into the
waking day.   I have seen you in the spring
forest, dancing and throwing your webs of sunlight to snare me; on moonlit mountains, laughing and calling; in the streets of crowded cities,
beckoning and disappearing in the crowd — and
everywhere I have fled from you, holding above
my head the sign of God's power in me, my
gift and my mission. — What use?   What use?
It has crumbled, and I do not care!

RHODA.

Oh, don't speak such words, I beseech you.
Let me go.   This must not, shall not be!

*She makes another attempt to escape.   He presses upon her
until she stands at bay.*

MICHAELIS.

You are all that I have feared and shunned and
missed on earth, and now I have you, the rest
is as nothing.

He takes her, feebly resisting, into his arms.

I know a place out there, high in the great

mountains.   Heaven-piercing walls of stone, a valley of trees and sweet water in the midst — grass and flowers, such flowers as you have never dreamed could grow. — There we will take our happiness.   A year — a month — a day — what matter?   We will make a lifetime of each hour!

RHODA.

Yielding to his embrace, whispers.

Don't talk.   Don't think.   Only — love me. A little while.   A little while.

The deep hush of their embrace is broken by a cry from within.   The young mother opens the hall door, in a distraction of terror and grief.

MOTHER.

Come here!   Come quick!

Michaelis and Rhoda draw apart.   He stares at the woman, as if not remembering who she is.

I can't rouse him!   My baby's gone.   Oh, my God, he's dead!

She disappears.   Rhoda follows, drawing Michaelis, dazed and half resisting, with her.   The room remains vacant for a short time, the stage held by distant singing.   Beeler enters from the kitchen.   There is a knock at the outer door, which he opens.   Littlefield, Culpepper, and Uncle Abe enter.

LITTLEFIELD.

Your man hasn't vamoosed, has he? Uncle Abe here says he saw the Indian boy slipping by in the fog.

BEELER.

Turns to the negro inquiringly.

Alone?

UNCLE ABE.

Mumbles half to himself.

'Lone. 'Spec' he was alone. Didn't even have his own flesh and bones wif 'im!

BEELER.

What's that?

UNCLE ABE.

Holds up his right hand, which he eyes with superstitious interest.

Put dis hyar han' right frough him!—Shore's you're bo'n. Right plum' frough 'im whar he lives.

CULPEPPER.

Mediæval! Alsolutely mediæval!

LITTLEFIELD.

Not a bit of it. It's up to date, and a little more, too.

CULPEPPER.

I'm astonished that you take this situation flip-
pantly.

LITTLEFIELD.

Not for a minute.   My bread and butter are at
stake.

Wickedly.

Yours too, you know.

*Mrs. Beeler enters, alone, from the hall.   She is in a state of
vague alarm.   Her husband hastens to help her.*

MRS. BEELER.

What is it?   What is the matter?   I thought
I heard —

*She breaks off, as a murmur of voices rises outside.   There
is a sound of stumbling and crowding on the outer steps,
and violent knocking.   The outer door is forced open, and
a crowd of excited people is about to pour into the room.
Beeler, the Doctor, and the Preacher are able to force the
crowd back only after several have made an entrance.*

BEELER.

Keep back!   You can't come in here.

*As he pushes them roughly back, excited voices speak to-
gether.*

VOICES IN THE CROWD.

Where is he? — They say he's gone away.   We seen his boy makin' for the woods. — Oh, it's not true!   Make him come out.

BEELER.

Curse you, keep back, I say!

Rhoda has entered from the hall, and Martha from the kitchen.   The two women support Mrs. Beeler, who remains standing, the fear deepening in her face.

A VOICE.

On the outskirts of the crowd.

Where's he gone to?

BEELER.

He's here.   In the next room.   Keep back! Here he comes now.

Michaelis appears in the hall door.   There is a low murmur of excitement, expectation, and awe among the people crowded in the entrance.   Beeler crosses to help his wife, and the other men step to one side, leaving Michaelis to confront the crowd alone.   Confused, half-whispered exclamations:

VOICES IN THE CROWD.

Hallelujah!   Emmanuel!

A NEGRO.

Praise de Lamb.

A WOMAN.

Above the murmuring voices.

" He hath arisen, and His enemies are scattered."

MICHAELIS.

Who said that ?

A woman, obscurely seen in the crowd, lifts her hands and cries again, this time in a voice ecstatic and piercing.

A WOMAN.

" The Lord hath arisen, and His enemies are scattered ! "

MICHAELIS.

His enemies are scattered ! Year after year I have heard His voice calling me—and year after year I have said, "Show me the way." And He showed me the way. He brought me to this house, and He raised up the believing multitude around me. But in that hour I failed Him, I failed Him. He has smitten me, as His enemies are smitten. — As a whirlwind He has scattered me and taken my strength from me forever.

He advances into the room, with a gesture backward through the open door.

In yonder room a child lies dead on its mother's knees, and the mother's eyes follow me with curses.

At the news of the child's death, Mrs. Beeler has sunk with a low moan into a chair, where she lies white and motionless. Michaelis turns to her.

And here lies one who rose at my call, and was as one risen; but now —

He breaks off, raises his hand to her, and speaks in a voice of pleading.

Arise, my sister!

She makes a feeble gesture of the left hand.

Rise up once more, I beseech you!

She attempts to rise, but falls back helpless.

BEELER.

Bending over her.

Can't you get up, Mother?

She shakes her head.

MICHAELIS.

Turning to the people.

Despair not, for another will come, and another and yet another, to show you the way.   But as for me —

He sinks down by the table, and gazes before him, muttering in a tragic whisper.

Broken!   Broken!   Broken!

CURTAIN

ACT III

ACT III

The next morning, just before sunrise. Both door and windows are open, and a light breeze sways the curtains. Outside is a tree-shaded and vine-clad porch, with balustrade, beyond which is a tangle of flowering bushes and fruit trees in bloom. The effect is of a rich warm dawn — a sudden onset of summer weather after a bleak spring.

Beeler, with Uncle Abe looking on, is busy putting up the pictures which he has taken down in the preceding act. Martha enters from the hall.

BEELER.

To Martha.

Is Mary up?

MARTHA.

Yes. Wants to go out on the porch and watch the sun rise, same as she's done every Easter morning since Seth died.

BEELER.

Won't hurt her, I reckon, bad off as she is. — A reg'lar old-fashioned, sunshiny, blossomy spring mornin' — summer here with a jump and fine growin' weather.

301

Pause.

All the same, sun might as well stay in China this Easter!

MARTHA.

Is that why you're tackin' up them fool pictures again?

BEELER.

Yes, ma'am. That's just why.   Religion!

MARTHA.

You wa'n't so sure yesterday, when you saw your wife stand up on her two dead feet and walk.

BEELER.

Well, she ain't walkin' now.

MARTHA.

No, she ain't, poor thing.

BEELER.

Natural cure, natural relapse.   Doctor says the new medical books explain it.

MARTHA.

Give it a name, maybe!

BEELER.
Bursts out petulantly.

You women don't want things explained, any more'n Abe here! You prefer hocus-pocus. And nothin' will teach you. Take Rhody! Sees Michaelis flunk his job miserable. Sees Mary go down like a woman shot, hands and legs paralyzed again, — Doctor says, for good, this time. And what does the girl do about it? Spends the night out yonder laborin' with them benighted sick folks, tellin' 'em the healer will make good. Lots of makin' good he'll do!

He points at the ceiling.

A fine picture of a healer he makes.

MARTHA.
Looking up.

Still as a stone! I'd rather have him ragin' round same as yesterday, like a lion with the epizoötic.

BEELER.

He's a dead one. Rhody might as well give up tryin' to make folks think different.

MARTHA.

Maybe Rhody holds she's to blame.

BEELER.

To blame?   To blame for what?

MARTHA.

For him a-peterin' out.

BEELER.

What's she got to do with it?

MARTHA.

Maybe she ain't got nothin' to do with it, and maybe she's got a whole lot.

BEELER.

Marthy, I don't want it to get out, but you're a plum' luny sentimental old maid fool!

Uncle Abe has been hovering, with superstitious interest, near the picture of Pan and the Pilgrim.   With side glances at it, he speaks, taking advantage of the lull in conversation which follows Beeler's outburst.

UNCLE ABE.

Mistah Beelah, 'scuse me troublin' you, but — 'scuse me troublin' you.

BEELER.

What is it, Abe?

UNCLE ABE.

It's purty brash o' me to be askin', but—Mista Beelah, fur de Lawd's sake give me that thar devil—pictuh!

BEELER.

What do *you* want with it?

UNCLE ABE.

Want to hang it up in my ole cabin.

His tone rises to one of eager pleading.

Mars Beelah, you give it to me! For Gawd's sake, say Ole Uncle Abe kin have it, to hang up in his ole cabin.

BEELER.

Well, if you feel as strong as that about it, Abe, take it along.

UNCLE ABE.

As he unpins it with feverish eagerness.

Thank ye, Mistah Beelah, thank ye.   I'll wo'k

fur ye and I'll slave fur ye, long as the worl'
stan's.   Maybe it ain't goin' to stan' much longer
aftah all.   Maybe de chariot's comin' down in
de fiery clouds fo' great while.   An' what'll yo'
ole Uncle Abe be doin'?   He'll be on his knees
'fore a big roarin' fire, singing hallelujah, an'
a-jammin' red-hot needles right plum' frough dis
heah black devil's breas' bone!   I'se got him
now!   I'll fix'm.

Shakes his fist at the print, as he goes toward the kitchen.

Put yo' black spell on the Lawd's chosen,
would ye?   I'se got ye.   I'll make ye sing,
" Jesus, my ransom," right out'n yo' ugly black
mouf!

Exit.   BEELER.

There's a purty exhibition for this present year
o' grace!   Thinks our friend Pan there has
bewitched the healer.

MARTHA.

Maybe he has!

BEELER.

Thought you said Rhody done it.

MARTHA.

Same thing, I reckon, by all that you tell about that Panjandrum and his goin's on!

BEELER.

Nonsense!

MARTHA.

If you're so wise, why do *you* think Michaelis petered out?

BEELER.

Couldn't stand the strain. Bit off more'n he could chaw, in the healin' line. — Never looked at Rhody.

MARTHA.

Looked at her till he couldn't see nothin' else, in heaven or earth or the other place.

BEELER.

You're dead wrong.   I tell you he never looked cross-eyed at Rhody, nor Rhody at him.   Doctor's more in her line. — By the way, did you give the Doctor a snack to stay his stomach?

MARTHA.

Done nothin' but feed him all night long. Seems to be mighty exhaustin' work to tend a sick baby.

BEELER.

Does he think it'll live?

MARTHA.

Not likely.   But he thinks he will, if fed reg'lar.
— What do you call that trance the baby's in?

BEELER.

Doctor calls it comy.   Spelled it out for me:
c-o-m-a, comy.

*Beeler goes out on the porch and disappears.   Martha con-
tinues her task of tidying up the room.   Michaelis enters
from the stair, carrying his hat and a foot-traveller's knapsack.   Martha regards him with curiosity, tempered now
by feminine sympathy with the defeated.*

MARTHA.

Good morning, sir.

MICHAELIS.

Tonelessly.

Good morning.

MARTHA.

Pointing at his hat and knapsack.

Hope you ain't off.   Don't mind sayin' the way
you acted was human decent, sendin' for Doctor
when you found the baby wa'n't dead, an' you
wa'n't no healer any more.

MICHAELIS.

Is it any better?

*Martha makes a disconsolate gesture, implying that there is
little or no hope. Michaelis turns away with bent head.
Annie enters from the kitchen. Michaelis holds out his
hand to her, and she takes it with shy hesitation.*

MARTHA.

Guess you'd like to know where Rhody is,
wouldn't you? She's where she's been all night,
—out yonder with the sick folks.

MICHAELIS.

What is she doing there?

MARTHA.

Feedin' 'em, first off, an' then heart'nin' of 'em
up. That's a purty hard job, I reckon; but it's
the way o' women when they feel like she does.

Michaelis sinks in a chair, drawing Annie to him.
Mrs. Beeler's bell rings; Martha goes out by the hall door.
Annie watches his bent head in silence for a moment.

ANNIE.

Are you ever going up again, on the rope?

MICHAELIS.
Not remembering.
On the rope?

ANNIE.

You know . . . the magic rope. — Ain't you ever going to climb up in the sky again?

MICHAELIS.

Recollecting.

Never again, Annie.   Never again.

ANNIE.

Have you got the rope still?

MICHAELIS.

No, I have lost it.

ANNIE.

Won't you ever find it?

MICHAELIS.

It can only be found by some one who will know how to use it better than I did.

ANNIE.

How better?

MICHAELIS.

By some one who can climb up, toward the sun and the stars, and yet never leave the earth, the cities, and the people.

ANNIE.

Then he'll have to take them up with him.

Michaelis nods for yes.

Gracious!

She runs to the porch door to meet Rhoda, who appears outside.

Cousin Rhoda! What do you think he says about the magic rope?

RHODA.

What, Annie?

ANNIE.

He says that first thing you know, everything will be going up in the air, towns and people and everything.

RHODA.

Does he?

ANNIE.

Runs out into the hall, balancing her arms above her head and gazing up laughingly.

Dear me! That will be very *tippy!*

Rhoda enters.

MICHAELIS.

You are here! The fear came over me, just now —

RHODA.

I could not go until I had told you the truth —
about myself — about us.

MICHAELIS.

You will tell me the whole truth, and I will
tell you the same.   But that will be for later.
Come!   Come away with me, into the new life.

RHODA.

A life rooted in the failure of all that life has
meant to you from the beginning!

MICHAELIS.

Until yesterday I did not know what my life was.

RHODA.

You do not know that, even yet.   You know it
now less than ever — what your life is, what it
means to you, what it means to the world.

MICHAELIS.

To the world it can mean nothing.   That is
ended.   But to us it can mean happiness.   Let
us make haste to gather it.   Come!

RHODA.

Where do you want me to go?

MICHAELIS.

Anywhere — to that place I told you of — high in the great mountains.

RHODA.

I was there last night.

MICHAELIS.

In your thoughts?

RHODA.

I was there, and saw all the beauty of it, all the peace.   But one thing was not there, and for lack of it, in a little while the beauty faded and the peace was gone.

MICHAELIS.

What was not there?

RHODA.

The work you have to do.

MICHAELIS.

That was a dream I could not realize.   I have striven, and I have failed.

RHODA.

Do you know why you have failed?

MICHAELIS.

Yes.

RHODA.

Tell me why.

MICHAELIS.

Because I have loved you more than the visions that came to me in desert places, more than the powers that fell upon me at the bedside of the sick, more than the spirit hands and spirit voices that have guided me on my way.

RHODA.

What of the sick and suffering out yonder, who are waiting and hoping against hope? What of them?

MICHAELIS.

I cannot help them.

RHODA.

Once you dreamed you could.

MICHAELIS.

Yes.   But that is over.

RHODA.

And who is to blame that that great dream is over?

MICHAELIS.

No one is to blame.   It has happened so.

RHODA.

Doesn't it seem strange that the love of a woman entering into your heart should take away such a dream as that?

MICHAELIS.

I do not question.   It is so.

RHODA.

But if your love had fallen, by some sad chance, upon a woman who was not worthy of love?

MICHAELIS.

What are you saying?

RHODA.

You know less than nothing of me.   You have not asked me a single question about my life.

MICHAELIS.

There was no need.

Rhoda.

There was need!   There was need!

Michaelis.

Be careful what you say.   Go on!

Rhoda.

In the first hour of our meeting, and all the hours of the next day, you swept me along and lifted me above myself, like a strong wind. I didn't know what you were. I didn't know why I was happy and exalted. It was so long since I had been happy, and I had never been as happy as that, or anything like it. Then, yesterday morning, came the revelation of what you were, like a blinding light out of the sky! And while I stood dazed, trembling, I saw something descend upon you like a shadow. You loved me, and that love was dreadful to you. You thought it was so because I was a woman and stole your spirit's strength away. But it was not that. It was because I was a *wicked* woman.

Michaelis.

Why do you call yourself a wicked woman?

RHODA.

Because I am so.

MICHAELIS.

I cannot believe it.

RHODA.

It is true.

MICHAELIS.

Is that why you wanted to go away?

RHODA.

Yes, I tried to go away. You wouldn't let me go.
Then I tried to tell you the truth. I knew why
I took your strength away, and I had nerved
myself to tell you why.   But you began to speak
— those wild words.   I could not resist you.
You took me in your arms; and all the power
of your soul went from you, and your life went
crashing down in darkness.
Long pause.

MICHAELIS.

Wicked?   A wicked woman?

RHODA.

I was young then, wild-hearted, pitifully igno-
rant.   I thought that love had come to me.

Girls are so eager for love. They snatch at the shadow of it. — That is what I did. — I am not trying to plead for myself. — Some things are not to be forgiven. — Somewhere in my nature there was a taint — a plague-spot. — If life is given me, I shall find it and root it out. I only ask for time to do that. But meanwhile I have done what I could. I have told you the truth. I have set you free. I have given you back your mission.

Dr. Littlefield enters, carrying his hat and medicine case. He looks sharply at Rhoda, then turns to Michaelis. His manner towards him is politely contemptuous, toward Rhoda it is full of covert passion, modified by his habitual cynicism and satire.

LITTLEFIELD.

To Rhoda.

Good morning.

To Michaelis.

Good morning, my friend. I understood that you sent for me, last night.

MICHAELIS.

I did.

LITTLEFIELD.

Glad to accommodate a fellow practitioner, even if he is in a side line. Some folks think your way of business is a little shady, but Lord, if they knew the secrets of *our* charnel-house!

MICHAELIS.

How did you leave the child?

LITTLEFIELD.

Done for.   I said I was worth a million of you in a case like this, but I didn't realize how far things had gone.   The next time, call me in a little sooner.

He writes on his note pad, tears out a leaf, and lays it on the table.

Mrs. Beeler will continue the old prescription, alternating with this.

He puts the note pad in his pocket, and turns to Rhoda.   He speaks in a tone which implies command, under the veil of request.

Will you walk a ways with me, Miss Williams?

RHODA.

Pale and trembling.

No.

LITTLEFIELD.

Pardon!   I must have a short talk.   It is important.

RHODA.

I cannot go with you.

LITTLEFIELD.

I think you had better reconsider.

MICHAELIS.

Astonished at his tone.

You have heard that she does not wish to go.

LITTLEFIELD.

Ignoring Michaelis.

I have no time to waste, and I shall not stop
to mince my words.   You are coming with me,
and you are coming now.

MICHAELIS.

To Rhoda.

Who is this man?

LITTLEFIELD.

Wheeling upon him angrily.

'Pon my honor!   "Who is this man?"   "Re-
move the worm!"   Decidedly tart, from a mir-
acle-monger in a state of bankruptcy.

MICHAELIS.

To Rhoda.

Is this the man you told me of?

RHODA.

Steadily.

Yes.

LITTLEFIELD.

To Rhoda, as he eyes Michaelis with dislike.

So you have called in a father confessor, eh?

To Michaelis.

Well, since the lady can't keep her secrets to herself, this *is* the man.   Very painful, no doubt, but these little things will happen.

To Rhoda.

I should have chosen a more secluded nook to say this in, but you're skittish, as I have learned to my cost, and likely to bolt.   What I want to say is, *don't* bolt.   It won't do you any good. — I've found you once, and I'll find you again, no matter what rabbit's hole you dodge into.

To Michaelis.

This ain't George Littlefield, M.D., talking now.   It's the caveman of Borneo.   He's got arms as long as rakes, and teeth that are a caution. — Look out for him!

MICHAELIS.

Holding himself in stern restraint.

Your arms and teeth are long enough, and eager enough to do damage, but they will not avail you here.   This girl is in other keeping, and I dare to say, better.

LITTLEFIELD.

In other keeping, eh?   Yours, I suppose.

MICHAELIS.

Yes, mine.

LITTLEFIELD.

Bless my soul!

He turns to Rhoda, pointedly ignoring Michaelis.

Look here, Rho, be sensible.   I'm tired of this hole of a town already.   We'll go west and renew our youth.   Country's big, and nobody to meddle.   You'll flourish like a green bay tree.

Rhoda turns distractedly, as to escape; he intercepts her.

Confound it, if you're so set on it, I'll marry you!   Say yes, and let John the Baptist here give us his blessing.   Speak up.   Is it a go? —Till death us do part.

MICHAELIS.

Death has already parted you and her.

LITTLEFIELD.

So? I feel like a reasonably healthy corpse.

MICHAELIS.

There is no health in you. Every word you
speak gives off corruption.

LITTLEFIELD.

Indeed! My advice to you is, make tracks for
your starvation desert. A parcel of locoed
Indians are about right for a busted prophet.

MICHAELIS.

What I am is no matter. What this girl is,
though you lived a thousand years, you would
never have the grace to imagine. She gave
you her young love, in childish blindness, not
knowing what she did, and you killed it idly,
wantonly, as a beast tortures its frail victim,
for sport. You find her again, still weak and
bleeding from her wounds, and you fling her
marriage, in words whose every syllable is an
insult. Marriage! When every fibre of her
nature must cry out against you, if she is
woman. Take your words and your looks from
her, and that instantly, or you will curse the

day you ever brought your evil presence into her life.

He advances upon him threateningly.

Instantly, I say, or by the wrath of God your wretched soul, if you have one, shall go this hour to its account!

LITTLEFIELD.

Backing toward the door, scared, but keeping his brazen tone.

All right. — I'm off. — Caveman for caveman, you've got the reach!

To Rhoda.

But remember, my lady, we're not quits by a jugful. You'll hear from me yet.

MICHAELIS.

She shall never hear from you, nor of you.

LITTLEFIELD.

In the door.

Last call, old girl! — Women!

He goes out, slamming the door behind him. Long pause.

MICHAELIS.

Poor child! Poor child!

RHODA.

I am sorry that you have had to suffer this.

MICHAELIS.

It is you who have suffered.

Martha enters from the hall, wheeling Mrs. Beeler in the invalid chair. She lies lower than in the first act, her manner is weaker and more dejected. Rhoda, whose back is turned, goes on as the two women enter.

RHODA.

I deserve to suffer, but it will always be sweet to me that in my need you defended me, and gave me back my courage.

Michaelis goes to Mrs. Beeler; she gives him her left hand as at first.

MRS. BEELER.

My poor friend!

Martha, resigning the chair to Rhoda, goes out. Mrs. Beeler looks up at Rhoda anxiously.

What were you saying when I came in?

As Rhoda does not answer, she turns to Michaelis.

Something about your defending her.—Against what?

MICHAELIS.

Nothing.   Her nature is its own defence.

MRS. BEELER.

Caressing her.

Ah, no! She needs help. She cannot bear it that this disaster has come, through her. It has made her morbid. She says things about herself, that make me tremble. Has she spoken to you — about herself?

MICHAELIS.

She has laid her heart bare to me.

MRS. BEELER.

That is good. Young people, when they are generous, always lay disaster at their own door.

She kisses Rhoda. The girl goes into the porch, where she lingers a moment, then disappears. Mrs. Beeler sinks back in her chair again, overtaken by despondency.

Isn't it strange that I should be lying here again, and all those poor people waking up into a new day that is no new day at all, but the old weary day they have known so long? Isn't it strange, and sad?

MICHAELIS.

I ask you not to lose hope.

MRS. BEELER.

Rousing from her dejection into vague excitement.

You ask me that? — Is there — any hope? Oh,
don't deceive me — now! I couldn't bear it
now! — Is there any hope?

MICHAELIS.

A half-hour ago I thought there was none.
But now I say, have hope.

MRS. BEELER.

Eagerly.

Do you? Do you? Oh, I wonder — I wonder
if that could be the meaning —?

MICHAELIS.

The meaning —?

MRS. BEELER.

Of something I felt, just now, as I sat there in
my room by the open window.

MICHAELIS.

What was it?

MRS. BEELER.

I — I don't know how to describe it. — It was
like a new sweetness in the air.

She looks out at the open window, where the spring breeze lightly wafts the curtains.

MICHAELIS.

The lilacs have opened during the night.

MRS. BEELER.

It was not the lilacs. — I get it now again, in this room.

She looks toward the lilies and shakes her head.

No, it is not the lilies either. If it were any-one else, I should be ashamed to say what I think.

She draws him down and speaks mysteriously.

It is not real flowers at all!

Song rises outside — faint and distant.

MICHAELIS.

What is it to you?

MRS. BEELER.

It is like — it is like some kindness in the air, some new-born happiness — or a new hope rising. Now you will think I am — not quite right in my mind, as Mat does, and Martha!

MICHAELIS.

Mrs. Beeler, there is such a perfume about us this beautiful Easter morning. You perceive it, with senses which suffering and a pure soul have made fine beyond the measure of woman. There is a kindness in the air, new-born happiness, and new-risen hope.

MRS. BEELER.

From whose heart does it rise?

MICHAELIS.

From mine, from Rhoda's heart, though she knows it not, from yours, and soon, by God's mercy, from the heart of this waiting multitude.

The song, though still distant, grows louder.
Mrs. Beeler turns to Michaelis and gazes intently into his face.

MRS. BEELER.

The light has come into your face again! You are — you are — Oh, my brother, what has come to you?

MICHAELIS.

I have shaken off my burden. Do you shake off yours. What is pain but a kind of selfishness? What is disease but a kind of sin?

Lay your suffering and your sickness from you as an out-worn garment. Rise up! It is Easter morning. One comes, needing you. Rise up and welcome her!

Mrs. Beeler rises and goes to meet Rhoda, entering from the porch.

RHODA.

Aunt Mary! You are walking again!

MRS. BEELER.

He told me to arise, and once more my dead limbs heard.

RHODA.

God in His mercy be thanked!

MRS. BEELER.

I rose without knowing what I did. It was as if a wind lifted me.

RHODA.

Yes, yes. For good, this time!

MRS. BEELER.

So different from yesterday. I was still weak then, and my limbs were heavy. Now I feel as if wings were on my shoulders.

She looks toward the outer door, and listens to the singing, now risen to a more joyful strain.

I must go out to them.

She turns to Michaelis.

Say that I may go out, and give them the good tidings of great joy.

MICHAELIS.

May the Lord be with you as you go!

To Rhoda, who starts to help her aunt.

Alone!

MRS. BEELER.

Yes, alone. I want to go alone.

She takes a lily from the vase, and lifting it above her head, goes out through the porch, which is now flooded with sunshine.

As she goes out she says:

The Easter sun has risen, with healing in its wings!

She crosses the porch and disappears.

RHODA.

I felt something dragging me back. It was Aunt Mary's spirit.

MICHAELIS.

No, it was mine.

RHODA.

Yours?

MICHAELIS.

My spirit, crying to you that I was delivered.

RHODA.

I delivered you.   That is enough happiness for one life.

MICHAELIS.

You delivered me, yes.   But not as you dream. Yesterday when the multitude began to gather, the thing I had been waiting for all my life was there, and I — because of you — I was not ready.   In that blind hour my life sank in ruin. — I had thought love denied to such as had my work to do, and in the darkness of that thought disaster overwhelmed me. — I have come to know that God does not deny love to any of his children, but gives it as a beautiful and simple gift to them all. — Upon each head be the use that is made of it!

RHODA.

It is not I — who — harm you?

MICHAELIS.

It is you who bless me, and give me back the strength that I had lost.

RHODA.

I?

MICHAELIS.

A little while ago you told me your life's bitter story. I tasted your struggle, went down with you into the depths of your anguish, and in those depths, — the miracle! Behold, once more the stars looked down upon me from their places, and I stood wondering as a child wonders. Out of those depths arose new-born happiness and new-risen hope. For in those star-lit depths of pain and grief, I had found at last true love. You needed me. You needed all the powers I had thrown away for your sake. You needed what the whole world needs — healing, healing, and as I rose to meet that need, the power that I had lost poured back into my soul.

RHODA.

Oh, if I thought that could be!

MICHAELIS.

By the mystery that is man, and the mercy that is God, I say it is so. —

Puts his hand on her head, and gazes into her face.

I looked into your eyes once, and they were terrible as an army with banners. I look again now, and I see they are only a girl's eyes, very weak, very pitiful. I told you of a place, high in the great mountains. I tell you now of another place higher yet, in more mysterious mountains. Let us go there together, step by step, from faith to faith, and from strength to strength, for I see depths of life open and heights of love come out, which I never dreamed of till now!

A song rises outside, nearer and louder than before.

RHODA.

Against your own words they trust you still.

MICHAELIS.

It was you who held them to their trust!

RHODA.

You will go out to them now.

MICHAELIS.

As he kisses her.

Until the victory!

The song rises to a great hymn, of martial and joyous rhythm.   They go together to the threshold.   They look at each other in silence.   Rhoda speaks, with suppressed meaning.

RHODA.

Shall it be — on earth?

MICHAELIS.

On the good human earth, which I never possessed till now!

RHODA.

But now — these waiting souls, prisoned in their pain —

MICHAELIS.

By faith all prisoned souls shall be delivered.

RHODA.

By faith.

MICHAELIS.

By faith which makes all things possible, which brings all things to pass.

He disappears.   Rhoda stands looking after him.   The young mother hurries in.

THE YOUNG MOTHER.

Ecstatic, breathless.

Come here — My baby!   I believe — I do believe —

She disappears.

RHODA.

Following her.

I believe.   I do believe!

The music rises into a vast chorus of many mingled strains.

CURTAIN

The Riverside Press
CAMBRIDGE · MASSACHUSETTS
PRINTED IN THE U.S.A.

THE POEMS AND PLAYS

OF

William Vaughn Moody

IN TWO VOLUMES

VOLUME II